GW00808987

INTEGRATED THINKING
THINKING
The New IT

Sue Pearson

COPYRIGHT

To Paul

CONTENTS

PREFACE

This book introduces a new way of thinking, Integrated Thinking or the New IT. Developing a new way of thinking means we have to change the way we use our brains, so before we change anything, we first need to know how our brains work.

We know that our brains adapt to accommodate changes in the outside environment, and that the brain also produces change in the world outside through the systems and societies it creates. What is less well known is that these systems and societies seem to reflect the brain's inner workings. This two-way process creates a mirror between inside and out, so that change in one is reflected in the other.

The brain is made up of many parts, each with its own role and focus in overall development. The New IT brings these different parts into a new framework for thinking. I use the word 'thinking' to include information, emotions, unconscious processes and the brain's internal integrating systems. This new framework or model can then be applied to social, political, global and spiritual development to see if we could create a more integrated and inclusive world.

Each section of the book addresses a different aspect of development and change. In Section 1 we look at the stages of human development to understand our present way of thinking better, and to create the basic New IT framework. Section 2 explores the links between human and social/political development, with particular reference to Britain today. In Section 3, we expand the New IT framework to include global development, and in the final Section, we will integrate the Mind and spirit into this new model.

Please note that I use the masculine to refer to a child to avoid the cumbersome him/her, and to a 'mother' to include a parent of either gender where appropriate.

SECTION 1

STAGES OF HUMAN DEVELOPMENT

"Changing government is not enough. We need to change the way
we think about ourselves and our role in society."
David Cameron

INTRODUCTION

This book introduces a new way of thinking, Integrated Thinking or the New IT, to help us respond appropriately to the crises and challenges we face in the world today. We begin by looking at what we think with - our brains - since before we change anything in our thinking, we first need to understand how the brain works. Changing our present way of thinking is not as easy as updating our mobile phones, but it is our brains' ability to adapt to and create change that has been the key to human survival and success. Thanks to neuroscience and psychology, the brain's workings can now be examined in more detail than ever before.

This first Section describes the stages of human development, and gives an overview of different elements in our thinking in order to clarify what we mean by 'our present way of thinking'. We will be focusing on the appropriate behaviour and responses for each stage, rather than on ideas about what is right or wrong.

The first chapter gives a brief outline of how the brain works, using straightforward language and simple diagrams. The technicalities of brain development are important to scientists and surgeons, but most of us need only the basics.

Chapter 2 looks at emotional development, drawing together knowledge from western psychology and eastern 'holistic' philosophy. In the third chapter, we will explore the unconscious, and Chapter 4 shows how inner integration is particularly critical at two key stages in life.

From this initial exploration, I will begin to create a framework for a new way of thinking, which I call Integrated Thinking, the New IT.

As we explore this inner world, we discover that the brain seems to use its internal systems and structures as a template for the social, political and global systems it creates. This means that inner and outer worlds can be integrated into an overall framework. Integrated Thinking differs from 'joined-up thinking' because of the extension of the framework to include this outer dimension.

This mirroring of inner and outer worlds is a complex process. It is not a simple case of cause and effect; for example, a child who is abused may continue to be abused in later relationships or he may turn the mirror the other way round and become an abuser in turn. The mirror can be one-way, distorted or reversed, for example when outer wealth compensates for inner impoverishment. Yet a better understanding of this mirroring process offers two opportunities for change: if we change the way we use our brains, we can change the world our brains create, while if we change the society we live in, then our brains change too.

1 BRAIN DEVELOPMENT

This chapter looks at how the brain works, using straightforward language and simple diagrams. In recent years there has been a huge increase in brain research. We know that the human brain is a single entity with many parts working together, and that the cells form interconnected neural networks. The different parts can be looked at separately just as organs in the body can be examined individually, although in the brain the parts are not so easy to identify. The brain has been compared to a Russian doll, with the more primitive parts nested inside later brain regions, but they all play a vital role in our lives and in the stages of human development. During human development, each part of the brain has a period of dominance relevant to a particular stage that then has to give way and play a supporting role to later evolving brain regions.

Deepak Chopra in *Superbrain* says the brain contains, "Roughly 100 billion nerve cells forming between a trillion to perhaps even a quadrillion connections called synapses. These connections are in a constant, dynamic state of remodelling in response to the world around you".

The brain has two main functions that use separate but interrelated networks: the first is to process information, and the second more important function is to use this information to help us progress as people. These two functions are also called head and heart, or IQ and EQ (see *Emotional Intelligence* by Daniel Goleman). In earlier times they were known as the Tree of Knowledge and the Tree of Life. It is not a question of 'all you need is information' or 'all you need is love': we need both.

Drew Western in his book *The Political Brain* explains how knowledge and feeling evolved alongside each other, and were designed by nature to work together. These two functions now seem to have grown apart, with information-processing taking the lead today, particularly in the West. The basis of the new way of thinking is to re-integrate the two brain functions in balance and in harmony, with information-processing supporting human development.

One of the brain's key characteristics is its ability to alter neural networks in response to changes on the outside, sometimes by adapting existing systems to new uses; in other words it recycles old parts for new purposes. This supremely useful flexibility, or *plasticity* as scientists call it, can cause problems if the environment to which the brain adapts is damaging, but given the right opportunities, this flexibility can also be used to re-wire the brain later.

In this chapter, we will see how the brain processes information, also known as its cognitive ability. We begin by looking at ourselves as if in a mirror, with right-to-right, and left-to-left (see Figure 1). Although people all have unique, individual faces, they also have basic features in common, such as the mouth, eyes, forehead and nose bridge. It is the same with the brain, for although each is unique, brains also have basic features in common. These features are more moveable in childhood, like the regions of the continents moved around the globe during the earth's formation.

My diagram shows the brain with four main parts and a connecting bridge at the central crossroads. This model offers more flexibility than the usual left/right division of the brain hemispheres. Carl Jung, the psychotherapist, believed the brain had a natural tendency to orientate itself through a foursome, like the points of the compass.

The four main parts have different ways of seeing the world, which can cause conflict if not integrated into a bigger picture. This reminds me of the story of four blindfolded men who were led to an elephant and asked to describe the whole animal from the bit they could touch: leg, tail, trunk or ear. They argued about who was right, but it was only when their blindfolds were removed that they could see the elephant as it really was, far more incredible that they could have imagined. By integrating the different ways of thinking instead of believing that one way is the only way, I hope to show that we too are far more incredible that we realise.

PRIMAL BRAIN

The four main parts or regions of the brain are the Primal Brain, the two Sides of the New Brain and the Forebrain, with the Wounded Body at the central crossing bridge. I will explain each of these names in turn, but each has its own way of processing information, its own purpose and role to play in the overall picture of human development.

THE HUMAN BRAIN

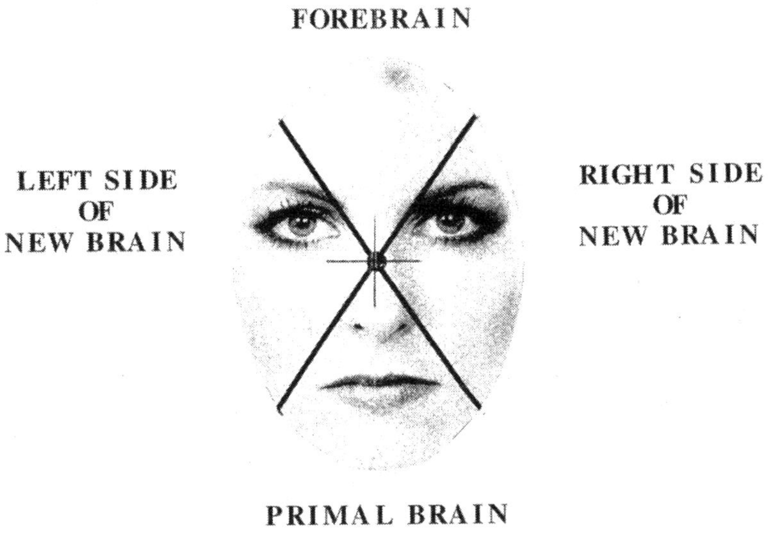

FOREBRAIN

LEFT SIDE
OF
NEW BRAIN

RIGHT SIDE
OF
NEW BRAIN

PRIMAL BRAIN

Figure 1 Four Parts of the Brain

As we move from one stage of life to the next, the part of the brain that dominates our thinking changes too, and so does our behaviour. Norman Doidge describes in *The Brain That Changes Itself* how, "The brain is divided into sectors, and in the course of development, each acquires a primary responsibility for a particular kind of mental activity". However, there can be problems if one part has become too dominant, and is reluctant to hand over primary responsibility to the next stage of brain development.

There are differences between male and female brains, and these have been shown to begin in the womb. Although some of these variations are often small compared with their similarities, they can have a major effect overall if in key places - rather like marginal seats can make big differences in elections to decide which party controls decision-making in Parliament.

The brain's neural networks create internal mental constructs based on its genetic inheritance and later experiences. Each stage completes part of the overall construct or mindset, and the foundation stage is of critical importance to later development.

Before birth the Gut Brain, a primitive instinctive brain in the baby's stomach, was the main processor of information and nutrition flowing via the umbilical cord from the mother's placenta, which also acts as a waste processor. In the womb a baby's development retraces the many stages of life on earth, from single cell to when mammals left the waters behind.

After birth the head brain is designed to take over the story of human development from the Gut Brain, which retains an island or *insula* in the brain to register the gut instinct which bypasses later, more rational development.

In his book, *The Decisive Moment,* Jonah Lehrer explains the link between individual and collective development. "The maturation of the human brain recapitulates its evolution, so that the first parts of the brain to evolve are also the first parts to mature in children."

The first part of the brain to develop in a baby's head and in the story of human development is the *brain stem*. It lies behind the mouth, and takes over from the Gut Brain after birth as the baby's main processor of information from the outside world. It was a French doctor, Michel Odent, who named this part of the brain the 'Primal Brain' in *Primal Health*, because it comes first after birth, and because it is inherited from our primitive and primate past. Its prime responsibility is for our physical survival.

The Primal Brain learns by repetition, copying, habit and images. Habit includes habituation, the brain's response to something it recognises. Initially when it meets something new, the Primal Brain is aroused or put on alert so it can focus attention in case of a potential threat, or in order to absorb new information. When it meets the same thing again, the alert response is reduced as the brain habituates to the stimuli and its attention response is then ready to move on to the next new thing.

It could be thought of as being rather like the lead headline story in the news, which after a while slips off the front page when it no longer catches our attention. This part of the brain can be overactive in those who constantly seek new thrills, but for others, too many new stimuli or threats in a short period of time can overwhelm the Primal Brain, especially in the early years.

Because the Primal Brain's prime concern is for the body's physical survival, it plays a central role in health throughout life, and can use the body to show when something is wrong elsewhere in the whole human system.

The primacy of its activities is not limited to early childhood, although that is when it is most dominant. Paul D Maclean in *The Triune Brain* claims that it is the Primal Brain that is responsible for the Four F's: Fight, Flight, Food and .... Sexual Intercourse. In today's world it seems as if some people's lives and many television programmes, computer games and films, are still dominated by these primal drives.

To do its work, the Primal Brain relies on two, very ancient, inherited systems. Firstly from the age of cold-blooded reptiles is the *reptilian core*, which I call the Serpent to give it a more easily recognisable image. It can be thought of as the brain's autopilot as it takes care of the body's automatic activities and processes, such as breathing, digesting, sleeping and so on. It is linked via the spinal column to the even more primitive Gut Brain.

The Serpent also takes over skills we learn later in life once they become automatic, for example, maths tables, typing or driving a car, so we can learn something new. This is a good example of the brain re-using older systems for new purposes. "Once a skill becomes automatic, we free our conscious thoughts for other matters", is how Cordelia Fine describes it in *A Mind Of Its Own*. The autopilot also takes over our thinking and behaviour when we are ill, tired or stressed: it is our default mode.

Its way of thinking is inherited from the competitive world of the jungle, where the predatory hunter preyed on the most vulnerable, such as the young, the sick and the old. We will see later how the Serpent's programmes can still dominate our thinking today, even when physical survival is no longer threatened.

Change does not come easily to the Serpent - think of crocodiles, unchanged since the Age of Dinosaurs. Changing old habits and moving on to new ways of thinking and behaving requires the other ancient survival mechanism of the Primal Brain, the *limbic system* from the age of warm-blooded mammals. It is called the limbic system from the word for a circle, because it encircles the more primitive Serpent. I call it the Emotional Wheel. It adapts to change more easily that the Serpent, and is even more important to human development than the invention of the wheel was in the history of the world. The Emotional Wheel has evolved from our mammal heritage, and we need to feel an emotional connection to the young, the sick and the old in order to care for them, rather than kill them in cold blood as prey.

The Emotional Wheel also connects us to nature, to the earth and animals and most importantly, to other people. Michel Odent in *Primal Health* tells how the Emotional Wheel can communicate with the brains of other humans and those of animals, and that stroking or being stroked stimulates the entire human system, and relaxes the Emotional Wheel. In later life, that can be the psychological stroking of applause, congratulations or sympathy, or the hug to say well done or welcome home.

TWO SIDES OF THE NEW BRAIN

In mankind's early journey, people moved out of the jungle and began creating societies. So a baby too moves from the survival mode of the Primal Brain to the more developed, socialising region of the brain in the *neocortex* or New Brain, retracing in his personal brain development the story of the human journey.

The *neocortex* is the part of the brain that sets people apart from their primate past. I call it the New Brain to distinguish it from the old Primal Brain. "It has been fatal when humans have employed their new brain capacities to enhance and promote old brain motivations", comments Karen Armstrong in *Twelve Steps To A Compassionate Life*. This happens when the Primal Brain does not hand over prime responsibility for development to the New Brain at the appropriate stage.

The New Brain is divided in two (see Figure 1), one on each side of the head like the eyes, and just as we need two eyes to work together to see clearly and in perspective, so we need both sides of the New Brain to work together to see both sides of a situation clearly and in depth, and to be able to see another's point of view.

We will look firstly at the Right Side of the New Brain, which plays a critical role in socialisation, building on the development of the Primal Brain's Emotional Wheel. Scientists have confirmed that it is the Right Side that is dominant in childhood.

The Right Side of the New Brain tends to be more actively developed in most women and communities, although not always. Its way of thinking is to see the world in terms of circles like the family circle, through connections such as the interconnected cycles of nature, and the importance of communication and relationships. It is in the family circle that a child first learns to care for others, by copying adults or through caring for pets or younger siblings, and to adapt to society's norms and authority. Social rules used to be called 'good manners', which encourage a child to think of others rather than himself. The Right Side can perform many tasks in parallel, switching between activities like having many computer windows open at the same time.

The Right Side of the New Brain likes to bring people together and thinks of 'me' as part of 'us', interdependent members of a group, tribe or union. It uses the language of meaning, including body language, and works by co-operation rather than competition. However, not wanting to stand out from the crowd can slide into passivity.

In global history, the East developed before the West, and the Right Side of the New Brain has tended to continue to be more dominant in the East where some still read from right to left. Richard E Nesbitt explores how Asians and Westerners think differently in *Geography Of Thought*. He quotes a student from China as saying, "You know, the difference between East and West is that I think the world is a circle, and you think it is a line".

However, many of those who live in the East are now crossing over between the two Sides and into an expansion of the role of the Left Side of the New Brain by copying western culture and development, which encourages personal independence, initiative and greater risk-taking, rather than conforming to the family's rules and more traditional ways. For in the West, it is the Left Side that has become the dominant way of thinking, particularly since the Industrial Revolution, and further enhanced through education, science, business and information technology.

The Left Side of the New Brain focuses on things and objects rather than people; it prefers to deal with one thing at a time, and likes to take things apart to analyse them rather than bring people together. The Left Side sees the world in terms of lines like the bottom line, divisions, facts and figures, personal choice and either/or logical thinking. Language is used to identify and delineate things, which can lead to a sense of ownership.

The Left Side of the New Brain is most often associated with the masculine and with men, although more and more women have developed their Left Side way of thinking through education, especially in the West. The Left Side of the New Brain likes to justify things, keeping things straight like justifying lines of typing on a page, but this skill can lead to self-justification of its actions. It tends to compartmentalise, dividing things up into separate boxes, and to initiate positive action - and to turn names into initials through the use of acronyms.

The focus of the Left Side is 'I' rather than other people, and this 'I' or ego development encourages individual independence. Since it thrives on challenge outside the comfort zone, learning to stand on your own two feet outside the security of the family circle is very much valued in Western society today, and to be free to choose one's marriage partner and career. But we need to be able to see the other Side's point of view to develop co-operation and compassion.

"Normally the two [Sides] are in constant communication. Each one not only informs the other of its own activities, it also corrects its mate, at times restraining it and balancing it. However, the Left [Side] can act like a bully, inhibiting and suppressing the Right", is how Norman Doidge views the relationship between the two Sides in his book *The Brain That Changes Itself*. This makes it sound like some marriages! It may make it easier to remember the differences between these two ways of thinking if we associate the Right Side with attachment and the Left with detachment.

The importance of these differences between the two Sides of the New Brain is that they are not just in our heads or personal lives; they have also been projected onto the outside world, because it seems that the human brain has used its own internal workings as a template for the systems and societies it has created. Those societies where Left Side thinking is dominant will tend to create systems that focus on things, lines, numbers, divisions and independence, whereas those societies where Right Side thinking is stronger will tend to emphasise family connections, holding things in common, people, dependency and conformity. However, we all have two Sides of the New Brain, and we need both Sides to work together like men and women in a marriage.

FOREBRAIN

When men and women come together, they can create something new and original - a baby - with genetic information coming from each parent. When both Sides of the New Brain come together, then something new and original can be created by the *prefrontal cortex* or Forebrain, with information coming from both Sides of the New Brain.

The Forebrain lies behind the forehead (Figure 1), and its way of thinking includes imagination, insight, hindsight, foresight and seeing the big picture. It plays a key role in planning, with its ability to foresee or predict consequences of intended actions by reference to past experiences and to the moral mental construct that first evolved during the socialising stage, called the superego in psychology.

In *Extreme Fear*, Jeff Wise explains the Forebrain's role as being, "To reflect, conceptualise, look into the future and predict the results of behaviour. But the [Forebrain's] systems require effort. The exercise of willpower is the [Forebrain] attempting to forcibly override a strong and deeply ingrained instinctive [Primal Brain]". The whole history of human and global development can be seen as the individual and collective maturation of the Forebrain over the more primitive Primal Brain.

There is a strong link in childhood between the Forebrain of imagination and the Primal Brain of the physical world, so that children confuse fantasy and reality, the symbolic with the physical. As the two Sides of the New Brain begin to develop, they create a bridge between them that reduces the Primal/Forebrain information traffic so that the Forebrain can begin the process of independent maturing in late adolescence and gain greater control over the Primal Brain, a process that continues throughout adulthood.

The Forebrain is sometimes called the brain's executive, but planning is only one of its many activities. By seeing one thing as 'like' another, it can extract underlying similarities or patterns to create abstract concepts or use these patterns in metaphor and analogy. The Forebrain is also the source of culture, music, arts, creativity, wisdom and spirituality. Spirituality is not the routine and rituals of religion, but an awareness of the interconnectedness of seemingly separate spheres, or the connection with levels we cannot see except with our mind's eye, for the Forebrain is also where the mind's eye or third eye of consciousness and conscience is thought to be located. The mind's eye can operate like a spotlight or television camera, concentrating a beam of light to call attention to a particular subject. Holding that focus takes energy and practice.

Ray Kurzweil in *The Age Of Spiritual Machines* tells also how scientists have found it is the Forebrain where the 'God Spot' is located, an ecstasy spot that can be lit up by whatever people worship - whether that is God, money, fame, sport or science. In *Letters To Lily*, Alan Macfarlane writes, "If anything is the new religion of the world it is football. More money, emotion and activity are now generated by sport and games than anything else on earth, except war".

The abuse of sex, drink and drugs takes the fast track to the Forebrain's mountain peak, but also the fast track down into an Underground Pit, which will be described in more detail in Chapter 3.

CROSSROADS

We have looked at the information-processing capacities of the four main parts of the brain separately but in reality they all work together, although not always in balance or harmony. The brain region where the four parts meet is called the *corpus callosum*, which can be translated as Wounded Body, but I will leave this phrase for later and refer to this central information hub in the brain as the Crossing Bridge. It runs from the bridge of the nose to the back of the head. Although women's brains, like their bodies, are on average smaller than men's, the Crossing Bridge is bigger in most women.

When I talk about 'crossing the bridge', I am referring to the changeover in balance between the Right Side and Left Side of the New Brain, so that one or the other plays a more dominant role in our thinking. The Crossing Bridge is the brain's main network interchange, a superhighway where information is integrated and distributed, with innumerable smaller connections in the overall network. The Crossing Bridge is also where control between the two Sides of the New Brain and the body cross over, so that the Right Side of the New Brain controls the left side of the body, and the Left Side of the New Brain controls the right side of the body. Information from the hands and eyes cross over here too.

There are two stages in life when the Crossing Bridge plays a critical role in development: firstly in adolescence, when a teenager crosses over from the family circle into the individualistic way of thinking associated with the Left Side of the New Brain, and the other is at midlife. These life stages are also accompanied by physical changes and by major re-wiring of the brain's networks, particularly in the Forebrain.

The other critical pathway through the Crossing Bridge is the top-down/bottom-up connection between the Forebrain and the Primal Brain, that links ideas and practice, imagination and reality. In children this link is called play, as they learn how things work through trial and error; in later life it is called testing a theory. This pathway also ensures that the maturing Forebrain is able to control the primitive urges of the Primal Brain, while habitual practices can be updated with new ideas - the basis of change and therapy. The Forebrain/Primal Brain pathway also contributes to the link between the mind's eye and the unconscious, a vital connection for insights in dreams and daydreams.

Development through the cycle of the four main parts within the brain does not stop in early adulthood but continues throughout life, and the revolving spiral creates a dynamic flexibility missing from the more usual left/right hemisphere split. Either/or divisions are typical of Left Side of the New Brain thinking, and so are hierarchies. Abraham Maslow in the 1950's developed his 'hierarchy of needs' theory, where more basic needs of security, food and shelter have to be met before moving up to higher needs such as esteem and individuation. However, in a spiral, stages neglected or underdeveloped earlier in life have the chance to catch up when the opportunity arises.

The four-part cycle is the way people mature and can respond to changing situations in the most appropriate way. Some may like to think of the brain's four main parts in terms of a car's gears that are changed in response to differing circumstances, with the Crossing Bridge as the gear change. There is some support for this analogy, for according to Norman Doidge, "The automatic gearshift, the *caudate nucleus*, is deep in the centre of the brain".

We are all aware of how we change the way we think and behave in different settings, such as business, social or sporting situations. In certain circumstances, the brain can fall back to lower levels of development, like choosing a lower gear, in response to the outside environment. This can be positive, as when a mother uses simple language to help a toddler develop speech; it can be relaxing when we float in warm water like an unborn baby; it can be arousing when activating the Primal 'mouth' Brain in kissing, or it can be damaging when a highly competitive environment encourages the Serpent's dog-eat-dog way of thinking.

CHAPTER REVIEW

We have now looked at the four main parts of the brain and their information-processing capacities, their importance to the stages of human development and how information is exchanged and integrated, like different agencies exchange information in society so that abused children do not fall through the net.

Although the stages of development appear to be universal and inbuilt, people do not develop at the same rate or develop all parts of the brain equally over time. What tends to happen is that we have one or two parts that are more developed than the others, both individually and collectively, depending on gender, genetics, upbringing and social norms. However, if the overdevelopment of one part comes to dominate all thinking, it can cause long-term damage - as with using only one gear in a car - and make individual and collective integration difficult.

If the different parts are not integrated, the imbalance causes inner conflict, as the underdeveloped or neglected parts struggle to have their contribution heard, like a repressed population in political decision-making. One way of dealing with the conflict is to reject the unwanted parts and project them onto others who become the 'enemy', or they can be used by something not under our conscious control, for nothing in nature is wasted. However, if one part becomes like a tyrant, and continues to be overdeveloped at the expense of all the other parts, which remain stunted, then the whole system can break down.

Having completed a first look at how the different parts of the brain process information, we will now turn our attention to the second, more important function of the brain, which is how the brain helps us progress emotionally, psychologically and morally as human beings, known to many as the Tree of Life.

2 EMOTIONAL DEVELOPMENT

We live in an Age of Information, but information alone is not enough to help us change. We also have to progress as people, and that means we have to integrate information-processing with the second, more important brain function of emotional and moral development, which is the next step towards Integrated Thinking.

I will be using two images to describe this function, a Wheel and the ancient Tree of Life, both of which have the concept of 'rings' as their basic idea.

THE EMOTIONAL WHEEL

We met the Emotional Wheel or *limbic system* of the Primal Brain in Chapter 1. It dates back to our mammal past, and encircles the earlier *reptilian core* or Serpent. Like the invention of the wheel in history, the Emotional Wheel plays a key role in human development. So why are emotions important? E-motion can be thought of as energy-in-motion, moving us to progress as human beings. To go back to the simple analogy of the parts of the brain being like the gears in a car: it is emotional energy that drives our 'motor' or motivation. We know that however good the gears in a car are, if we have no fuel, we are going nowhere.

The fuel that drives the Emotional Wheel has been called over time by many names, such as the energy of life, love, light, prana, chi, the vital force, the living stream and so on. Michel Odent sees a brain, "Which is constantly rhythmic and pulsating, giving a new vision to what ancients called 'vital energy'".

I am again using a simple diagram in Figure 2 of a circle and a cross as a visual aid to explore very complex, interrelated systems. According to Chinese tradition, the four basic emotions (or elements in acupuncture) are anger, fear, grief and compassion. The emotional energy has to flow through all the four basic emotions to complete the cycle and move the energy to higher brain levels. The four 'spokes' of the Wheel can operate as independent smaller wheels, and one emotion can spill over into another or come to dominate the whole Wheel.

EMOTIONAL WHEEL

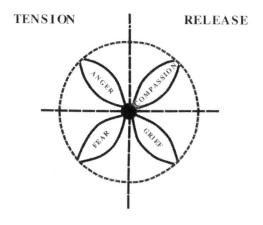

Figure 2 Emotional Wheel

This overspill can distort the Emotional Wheel and our thinking, because ALL emotions are essential for well-being and growth. It is important to emphasise this as some cultures or families only 'allow' the expression of certain emotions, or the emotions are divided up between genders or family members, so that their Wheels become entangled and difficult to separate. If one emotion is neglected or if one comes to dominate, the Emotional Wheel becomes unbalanced and progress is difficult, or even delayed. We saw a similar effect if one part of the brain comes to dominate, while others are neglected.

As the energy flows round the Emotional Wheel, it creates an energy field or personal space around us, rather like an electric fence around a house. We can all sense when others enter this field, even when we cannot see or hear them. Anyone who has worked or lived in other countries will also know that different cultures have their own sized personal spaces, so that each nationality will only feel comfortable if others keep to what is the 'safe' distance for them, making some back off and others to come closer.

Many people have very clear boundaries, but the boundaries of some are very fuzzy and their Wheels can merge with those of others, for example in childhood, co-dependency, mob situations or in some forms of mental illness. Deepak Chopra calls this merging, "Emotional contagion, in which one is not aware of whether the emotion belongs to oneself, or has been absorbed by contact with a stronger personality or the crowd."

Children have a particularly bright energy around them called innocence. It is a very attractive source of energy for a certain kind of predator. Forcible entry, such as rape, breaks through this barrier, and makes it vulnerable to further penetration, like a physical wound on the body.

Since the Emotional Wheel is part of our mammal heritage, when we look at animals we see them behaving in ways we associate with emotion, such as the compassionate understanding of dogs towards those who are blind or are in danger, or in the way elephants stand over their dead as if in grief. "Elephants live in communities and bury their dead. Their intense burial rituals include week-long vigils over the body, and they revisit the site for years afterwards", observes James Bruges in *The Big Earth Book*.

Emotional energy in people, however, is about more than behaviour. It is the foundation for human psychological, moral and spiritual growth, it is critical to the decision-making process and to change, and it is essential to attaching meaning to memory.

Scientists have found that the way we feel about something when making decisions is at least as important as information, facts or figures. Those unfortunate people whose brains are damaged so that they cannot feel their own emotions or those of others, can make decisions without reference to moral considerations. "People with [Forebrain] injury find it easier to make an emotionless decision about killing", reported *The Times*, 22 March 2007.

It is through their Emotional Wheels that people connect with one another. In mothers and babies, this means that their Wheels and brains can link as if they are part of a single system. The baby cries, her breast milk starts to flow; the mother smiles, the baby mirrors her actions. It is through the recently discovered 'mirror cells' in the brain that people seem to be able to feel what they see others feeling. This mirroring is the basis of caring and compassion, relationships and social engagement, and the emotional response to theatre and film.

At first, a mother will process a baby's emotions through her own Emotional Wheel, using her compassion to create a single emotional network. During his childhood and adolescence their Wheels gradually separate, although some adults continue to 'dump' their unprocessed emotional output onto others, overloading those with whom they have an emotional connection while freeing up their own Wheel.

The look of love flowing through a mother's eyes activates the mirror cells in a baby, as he absorbs her image of himself as loved and lovable, particularly if associated with the aroused pleasure of body-contact during feeding, and so the process of feeling connection with others begins.

Anger and fear, the Serpent's fight-or-flight response, cause arousal and tension on one side of the Emotional

Wheel, but it is grief and compassion on the other side which completes the cycle by releasing or relieving the tension with the less familiar tend-and-befriend response. In between is a pause button, a freeze response in the face of an overwhelming threat. Tension includes at-tention, so that focusing the Forebrain's spotlight has to be followed by release - like children's release of energy at playtimes after paying close attention in class.

The range of each emotion is very wide, so that anger can extend from mild annoyance to fury, fear can range from uncertainty to being petrified, and so on. The stronger the emotion, the faster that inner wheel turns, the more demands it makes on the body, and the more difficult it is for more mature parts of the brain to intervene.

So what can stop the Emotional Wheel of the Primal Brain from turning and so prevent the energy from moving on to higher brain levels? The Wheel can become blocked when the tension or arousal on one side is not released or relieved on the other side. Tension can be released naturally by taking physical action or in relaxation, talking, sleep, exercise or sex for example, or it can be released in blood, sweat or tears - your own or the blood, sweat or tears of others, abusively reversing those mirror cells so that others express what you feel.

Like all forms of energy, emotional energy does not disappear, so it has to go somewhere. The relief felt by a person who uses anger to get his own way, so that his victim expresses fear and grief, is usually temporary before the tension builds up again against the block. This form of vicarious release is a major source of pain and conflict.

Another way of releasing the energy if it does not complete the cycle is for it to flow out of the Serpent's fight-or-flight response of anger and fear, and down the S-bend into an Underground Pit, which we will explore further in Chapter 3. This can have the effect of sending the Emotional Wheel into reverse, down the evolutionary path to earlier brain development.

Grief is not just about crying, it is also about loss. If the brain does not feel the emotional pain of losing, it does not learn by its mistakes. Grief also means letting go the anger and fear of the past, and grieving for what is missing in our lives. To see what we might be missing, we need to follow the upward path of emotional development and climb the Tree of Life.

TREE OF LIFE

The Tree of Life is a more familiar image to those in the East and Middle East. It uses the idea of rings of growth to show how a tree has weathered the storms of the past to reach maturity. This inner Tree starts as a hidden seed in the womb, curled up, gradually unfolding and breaking through the barrier to grow and stand tall.

Imagine this inner Tree growing as a person grows, emotionally, psychologically and morally. Its roots go deep into the earliest, hidden beginnings in the Gut Brain. The trunk is the spine leading to the *brain stem* and its branches are in the brain. As the brain makes more connections, so it flourishes, just like the branches of a tree. Scientists even call these brain connections *dendrites* from the word for 'branch'. We use the same word for different areas of knowledge, with the branches of learning tending to separate, but it is possible they, like the many diverse forms of language, were once more closely connected.

If it is to bear fruit, a tree has to be pruned from time to time, and so it is with the brain, especially those routes that carry little traffic, in the same way that underused bus routes are cut back. We now know that a particularly strong pruning happens at critical stages in the brain's development, including immediately before birth, during adolescence and in midlife, which could be compared with the drastic cutting back of unproductive railway lines by Dr Beeching in the 1960's. Storms of tears in grief can be a way of pruning the dead branches, breaking connections that have outlived their usefulness, like storms bring down a tree's dead branches.

CLIMBING THE TREE

So how do we climb the Tree of Life? Diagram 3 overleaf (and in colour on the back cover) shows entwining spirals around a central core and has similarities with the symbol for healing, the Kabbala tree, the chakras of yoga or the Native American medicine wheel, but it also integrates the different stages of brain development with personal growth.

At the base of the Tree of Life is the Primal Brain's Emotional Wheel. If the emotional energy completes its cycle at this level, the energy can flow up into the socialising and individualising New Brain to feed the Tree of Life. Here the emotion of anger becomes the more mature feeling of justified or righteous anger, fear develops into respect, grief into regret and compassion becomes empathy, the essential qualities of psychological growth in an individual and of democracy in a society.

Steven Pinker quotes Jeremy Rifkin as saying, "Human evolution is measured not only by the expansion of power over nature, but also by the intensification and extension of empathy to more diverse others across broader domains of time and space. The growing scientific evidence that we are a fundamentally empathetic species has profound and far-reaching consequences for society and may well determine our fate as a species."

However, if the Emotional Wheel is unbalanced, then the higher levels of emotional development will be too. If the New Brain is unbalanced because the Left Side is dominant and the sense of 'I' or ego is overdeveloped, then the Left Side can use its skills to turn righteous anger into self-justification, demand respect and block regret so it does not feel the pain of loss or losing. Cordelia Fine describes this process in *A Mind Of Its Own*. "The [overdeveloped Left Side] biases, discounts, misinterprets, even makes up evidence - all so it can retain that satisfying sense of being in the right. The same kind of tricks that keep us bigheaded, also underlie our tendency to be pigheaded".

I call this overdeveloped sense of ego 'the Mighty I'.

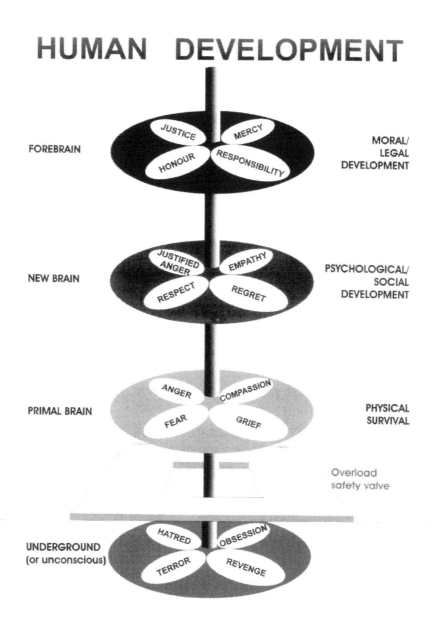

Figure 3 Tree of Life/Human Development

At a later stage of maturity, the emotional energy reaches the Forebrain, where justified anger becomes a sense of justice, respect becomes honour, regret becomes responsibility and empathy becomes mercy, the highest aspirations in law and morality. As with the Primal Brain's Emotional Wheel, the range of these feelings and senses is very wide, encompassing many concepts.

I mentioned earlier that there is a very strong link in childhood between the Forebrain and the Primal Brain, so that children's sense of what is fair can be very acute, but "it's not fair!" is often based on a misunderstanding that 'equal' means 'the same'. This has to develop in maturity to include a deeper understanding of more complex arguments of fairness and equality found in law and political reality.

If the Tree is unbalanced, then calls for justice are not moderated by the quality of mercy, and can even be a cover for revenge. "It is not just reason that separates us from the other animals, but the advanced nature of our emotions, especially our social and moral emotions", is how Jean Twenge and Keith Campbell see it in *The Narcissism Epidemic*. This maturity requires hard effort and sustained attention, and scientists have found that even a slight drop in blood sugar levels can affect the Forebrain's ability to function, so good nutrition plays an important role in Forebrain use and development.

It is the use of the adult Forebrain through the development of both Sides of the New Brain that controls and redirects the energies of the Primal Brain. The mature Forebrain is also the key to personal and historical development and to Integrated Thinking.

Tests with children have shown that, if they can delay instant gratification by resisting the attraction of a single sweet in front of them for a period of time in return for two sweets later, they are the most likely to score highly in emotional development tests and to succeed later in life. Even at that early age, their Forebrain is already taking over from the 'now, now, now' of their Primal Brain.

In acupuncture, the central core of the four emotions is fire, or perhaps 'passion' is a more familiar term. There is the physical pleasure of the Primal Brain's sexual passion, the incandescent fire of fury or jealousy, the glow of love and enthusiasm, and the sacred joy of the Forebrain's spiritual passion, familiar from the depictions of saints and martyrs. More down to earth, however, the youthful energy of sexual passion used to be put to work by diverting it to develop 'character', but this seems to have fallen out of fashion.

Figure 3 of the entwining spirals around a central core integrates the two functions of the brain - how we process information and progress as people - with the stages of human development. It also reflects many philosophies, for example, it brings together the two biblical trees from the Garden of Eden, the Tree of Knowledge and the Tree of Life. From a different branch of learning, Anthony Steven in his book on Jung describes how Jung saw development not as a simple, linear process, but as a spiral with progressive ascents and regressive descents, falling back to earlier levels of development. Today, scientists have also discovered that decision-making is very much affected by a person's level of emotional development.

DECISION-MAKING

It does indeed appear that emotions are essential to good decision-making. Jonah Lehrer states that, "It is only after the emotions have already made the moral decision that the rational circuits in the brain are activated. At its core, moral decision-making is about empathy". Antonio Damasio in *Descartes' Error* tells of a patient with emotional brain damage that affected his decisions even though information-processing such as memory and language were preserved. "The decision-making defect appears when a choice occurred. He was unable to choose effectively. I began to think the cold-bloodedness of his reasoning prevented him from assigning different emotional or moral values to different options, and affected his decision-making."

However, there are situations when this kind of moral decision-making is difficult for people even if they do not have brain damage. It is when people are tired, stressed, socially isolated or in a competitive environment that the Primal Brain takes over, with its focus on survival and 'just getting through the day', rather than considering moral consequences.

In *Wilful Blindness* Margaret Hefferman talks of Stanley Milgram's insight that when people feel overloaded, they restrict their social and moral involvement. Empathy demands a lot of emotional and mental energy, so people's overload is eased if they limit it, and that allows them then to continue working or pushing themselves on auto. "In very competitive environments where you're under a lot of stress", she writes, "and a lot of cognitive overload [ie too much information-processing], you won't even necessarily see that there is a moral consideration".

The effect of cognitive overload in the age of information is very real, yet those who do not invest emotional and moral energy into decisions can appear more confident about their decisions and even emerge as leaders. However, decisions made without a moral dimension are thought to be behind some of the present crises and challenges we now face.

If this is the effect of cognitive overload, it is not a reassuring thought for those entrusted with making decisions, such as politicians, overworked doctors and nurses, tired parents, those in competitive positions of power or those caught up in the culture of long working hours. Neither does it create confidence in those who have to deal with the effects of those decisions.

We need to make sure that the decisions we make, and those made on our behalf, are based on this new understanding of how the brain works and the role of the autopilot, and to understand how important it is to integrate emotional and cognitive development and make greater use of our Forebrains.

CHAPTER REVIEW

In this Chapter, we have looked at emotional development, and its role in individual and social progress. We have also integrated emotional and information-processing development into a model that has links with the knowledge and images from other cultures and times. In addition, we have seen how the latest scientific research emphasises the role of the emotions in our decision-making process, particularly those that are associated with the higher reaches of the Tree of Life.

The next stage is to look at what lies beneath the Tree of Life. Just as we cannot understand our planet unless we examine what is hidden beneath our feet, nor our history if we do not explore earlier civilisations, so we cannot understand ourselves unless we examine what lies beneath our awareness. We now understand how non-visible forces such as gravity act on the earth: in the next chapter, through the use of imagery and analogy, I want to reveal some of the non-visible forces acting on human development.

3 THE UNCONSCIOUS

The unconscious is a mysterious world that has profound effects on our lives. We begin our exploration of the unconscious by looking at what we mean by the word 'conscious'. It can be applied to the physical body to describe a person whose eyes are open and who is aware of what is happening around them. 'Conscious' can also be used in a psychological sense to describe a person whose inner eye is open, aware of what is happening around and within them, and crucially knows that he is aware. No longer the passive receiver of the Forebrain's spotlight like a television viewer, he has become the cameraman behind the lens, directing the spotlight for himself. So being 'un-conscious' means we are un-aware, either physically or psychologically.

The unconscious itself is a vast store of individual and collective knowledge that is usually kept hidden, partly because the conscious brain can only deal with a limited amount of knowledge at a time. In addition to storing inherited information, the unconscious holds the basic programmes of the whole potential of human development because a baby is not born as a blank slate, contrary to earlier theories. The unconscious contains stock characters in search of a place at certain stages in our lives, called stereotypes or archetypal figures by psychologists. Some of these archetypes were dramatised by Pirandello in his play *Five Characters in Search of an Author.* They were also visualised in the myths of gods and goddesses of the ancient worlds, and also in the supposedly seven basic life scripts that appear throughout literature.

Myths are far more than stories - they are prototypes of human behaviour and development, a primitive form of psychology. The stock characters are not only seen in many roles in theatre and film, they are also very important at critical points in human development. For example, adolescents in the West today try out 'roles' for themselves, or look to people outside the family circle as role models, before developing their own unique, individual identity and that awareness of 'I' or ego. At the same time they have to discard or neglect aspects of themselves (or their parents) that do not fit into this new model.

In history, this same individualising process happened when the gods and goddesses of the ancient worlds, possessing positive and negative aspects, were superseded by the concept of the one all-good masculine God of the great I AM, and the feminine and negative aspects were rejected, neglected or denied.

It is the unconscious that stores people's underused, overused, neglected or rejected aspects, their hidden memories and uncompleted developmental stages and tasks, until they can be integrated at a later stage. To give a recognisable image to this particular role of the unconscious, I will call it the Underground Pit. It lies beneath the Tree of Life and the automatic programming of the Primal Brain and it is the contents of this Underground Pit that can give the unconscious its negative image.

ON AUTO

The Underground Pit, so critical to human survival, is mostly under the control of the Primal Brain's autopilot, the Serpent. The Serpent can override the more developed parts of the brain in response to challenges to our survival. When people feel threatened, the Serpent of the Primal Brain reacts automatically with the fight-or-flight response, arousing anger and/or fear. If the tension is not released through action or through the Emotional Wheel, it can create a chemical overload in the brain we call stress.

To reduce the stress levels, the Primal Brain can adapt or habituate to the threats so that they become the norm, or the unreleased overload can be stored in the Underground Pit of the unconscious. Both responses, either separately or together, ensure our survival, particularly when we are young and have fewer options for releasing an emotional overload. Later in life we have other resources with which to respond to threats, such as removing ourselves from potentially harmful situations, negotiating skills or the law, but these require the use of a developed Forebrain and access to the legal system.

However, if the underground anger and fear is fed over time by more threats and emotional overload, the emotional energy can become twisted, so that anger breeds into venomous hatred, and fear twists itself into terror, working against change, activating negative and earlier levels of brain programming (see Figure 3). This will be explored further in Section 4. In the Underground Pit, other emotions can become twisted too so that unreleased grief can turn into grievance or revenge, and compassion into obsession which includes all forms of addiction.

The Underground Pit has been likened to the criminal underworld, a world of fantasy, nightmare and violence, mostly unseen but undermining the world above. It is a place where not only emotions are twisted, but where truth too can be twisted into lies and deceit. It must be clearly understood, nevertheless, that this overload storage began as a safety valve survival mechanism, part of the brain's automatic programming. One of the aims of Integrated Thinking is to re-integrate its contents and some of the released stored energy into the bigger picture of human development.

TRAPDOOR

The Primal Brain has strong links with the unconscious, and I have referred to the dominance in very young children of the Primal Brain, but this weakens as the New Brain begins to take over more responsibility.

Until this stage, a child's memories are unconscious, which is why most people's first conscious memories are after the age of two years old. The previous fluidity between the inside and outside world, between fantasy and reality, begins to become more clearly defined and separated as the unconscious is confined to a more restricted role.

Later, the Primal Brain itself will have to give way to more developed parts of the whole human system. But even if these early memories and experiences are unconscious, they form the unseen foundations for later mental constructs and development, as critical to future personal stability as the unseen foundations of a house.

As part of the handover to more evolved parts of the brain, and in order to keep the Underground Pit confined and not allowed free range, the Serpent of the Primal Brain must swallow its pride - and tail - and join forces with the unbroken Emotional Wheel, so that the emotional energy can flow up the Tree of Life and not down the S-bend into the Underground Pit. In some cultures, the image of the Serpent swallowing its tail was known as the Orobouros.

For most people, this subsuming of the Serpent within the Emotional Wheel helps create a trapdoor, an imaginary 'thin blue line' over the Underground Pit. For others, however, the door remains open or is only covered by a flimsy, fuzzy web, so that the Underground Pit continues to play a dominant role in their lives, distorting fact and fantasy, twisting reality into a violent underworld.

Some caught in this world are mentally ill, or are psychopaths who hide behind a mask of normality, while others seem to be caught up in acting out one of the unconscious' prewritten scripts: the all-powerful father figure, the helpless victim, the wicked seductress and so on. People can also be seduced into entering the Underground Pit through a portal where, like gateways to Internet pornographic sites, there is often a teaser. Religions call these traps temptations: same idea, just different branches of knowledge with different languages.

What can keep the trapdoor closed, so that the energy flows up the Tree of Life, or is only opened in order to release the contents of the Underground Pit safely?

One way is through the power of the word, which takes what is unconscious and makes it conscious. "Labelling emotions calms over-excited centres, and imaging studies have shown that this is what happens in psychotherapy", explains John Arden in *Rewire Your Brain*.

There is one particular word that releases the tension and arousal of the Serpent's anger and fear into the grief and compassion on the other side of the Emotional Wheel, so that the energy can then flow up the Tree of Life and not down into the Underground Pit. And that word is:

"Sorry".

This word, along with "please" and "thank you", is learnt in childhood as part of the awareness of other people and their needs, but sometimes "sorry" is the hardest word to say, especially if the 'I' of individuality has grown too large and turned into the self-justifying Mighty I. Yet "sorry" is the word that will turn the Emotional Wheel in the right direction to help us progress as people.

It is important that the word is said. Words activate the Left Side of the New Brain, taking what is unconscious and bringing it to the light of conscious awareness so it can be seen and can no longer be denied. It is similar to having television cameras turn their spotlight onto a particular situation, or when perpetrators are named in financial or sex scandals. It is then difficult to ignore the knowledge and we feel something has to be done.

Once the grief, regret and responsibility have been acknowledged, then it is time for compassion to step in, especially in the more advanced forms of empathy and mercy. When the Serpent is more closely linked in with the Emotional Wheel, the trapdoor entrance to the Underground Pit is more secure.

GOING DOWN

When the emotional energy does not complete its cycle around the Emotional Wheel, however, it can go down the Serpent's S-bend, through the trapdoor and into the Underground Pit of the unconscious. Here emotions can become more like toxic emissions, tapping into deeper, darker reserves. This Pit is made up of many layers, and the deeper the emotional energy falls, the more it is twisted into the darker aspects of human development, which used to be called the seven deadly vices.

This twisting mechanism, however potentially destructive later in life, does have a role in earlier stages of survival. Imagine a child who is jealous of a father, missing for many of the war years, who returns and comes between the boy and his too-close relationship with the mother. The boy's anger threatens to overwhelm his fragile identity, and the fear of reprisal is so great it risks his security and survival. To protect him from this threat, the unconscious twists the anger and jealousy so that they seem to be coming not **from** him but **to** him from his parents, whom he now sees as wanting to kill him, rather than the reverse. This may buy him temporary relief, but long term anxiety and later relationship difficulties.

Delusions are inappropriate mental constructs from earlier stages of development, or from the Underground Pit; for example the baby-belief that his needs will be met without having to ask can continue into adulthood. Appropriate for a baby, disastrous in a later relationship or in a tyrant.

The Underground Pit also includes programmes that have their place in the body's overall development, but which can be misapplied when used against people. For example, the Gut Brain's programme of breaking food up in the intestines and discarding what it does not need is absolutely essential to human survival, but when used as a programme against people in pogroms, scorched earth policies and ethnic cleansing, it causes untold damage. We will come back to this important subject several times in this book.

Breaking things up, fragmenting or disintegrating them can be important, like breaking connections in the brain ensures its flexibility to respond to new information, but it can become a force in opposition to integration rather than a necessary part of the whole picture.

In storing the unused or overused waste energy, the Underground Pit is only doing its job, like a waste disposal site. The purpose of developing conscious awareness is to take back as much as possible from the Pit and recycle it. When the Underground Pit itself is overloaded with wasted energy, the level of inner pollution rises, and the Pit finds it harder to recycle what is being stored. It is a similar picture in the outside world where levels of pollution are rising, and the earth's reprocessing systems are under pressure. However there is also a call for new uses to be found for waste products through recycling, reflecting a positive mirroring between the inner and outside worlds.

When the deeper, darker levels of the Underground Pit do burst through in corruption, sadism and destruction, it can be like earthquakes or volcanoes breaking through the weak spots in the earth's surface to reveal earlier stages in the earth's history. One problem today is that the more is stored away, the more we hand over to the autopilot and the Underground Pit, and so we waste that most precious resource - our human potential.

GATEKEEPER

We have seen that as people mature, they create their own unique identities from multiple possibilities, leaving other elements at a less developed stage. The Underground Pit stores them in their more primitive state until they can be re-integrated at a later stage, for example in relationships, in therapy or during crises. These initially unwanted aspects are not necessarily negative; for example, in a harsh or dysfunctional upbringing, a child may have to deny qualities such as sympathy or tenderness or his artistic skills in order to survive.

These underdeveloped elements, however, are not easy to contain and can demand attention by becoming disruptive and disturbing. In psychology, these hidden or shadow aspects can lead to personality disorders, while in theology they were called demons.

The discarded fragments of human potential are usually kept below our conscious awareness, although it takes energy to hold them back. Tradition has it that there is a gatekeeper at the trapdoor entrance to the Underground Pit that allows them out or back in.

The image for the gatekeeper to this underworld used to be the devil. Stephen Batchelor, in his book *Living With The Devil*, states that, "To be fully human entails coming to terms with a diabolical power that seems to stand in the way of our realising meaning, truth and freedom. Now that the powers stockpile weapons of mass destruction, contaminate the earth with their feverish industry, release floods of images to trigger insatiable desires, treat animals and humans as commodities and functions of the market, the devil must be grinning from ear to ear".

If the idea of a devil and demons seems too far-fetched in today's world, there is a subtler, more familiar image we could use instead. This kind of gatekeeper is more like a smooth-talking spin-doctor with his apparatchiks, the prince of darkness who twists the truth just a quarter turn. It says things like, "Everyone does it". "Nothing to do with me". "I am always right". Or even, "You can have whatever you want right now."

Cordelia Fine likened the gatekeeper to a butler, indispensable but devious, or perhaps even given to blackmail as in the 1960's film *The Servant*.

Its silky, devious or threatening voice is hard to resist, and it is easy to fall into its trap, but there is another voice we can listen to, the voice of consciousness and conscience in our Forebrain, so long as it is not drowned out by the vociferous demands of the Primal Brain and the Underground Pit.

CHAPTER REVIEW

We have explored some of the core aspects of the usually hidden world of the unconscious. We have seen how some of its programmes can be misused or be projected onto the world outside. I hope I have also shown that, rather than working against progress, its roles and activities can be consciously integrated into a larger picture of human development. The Underground Pit in the unconscious can spill out in times of great change, when cracks appear on the surface; for example when couples split up during a divorce, and also during periods of social upheaval. It can be a prelude to changes in our way of thinking, just as when anger and frustration spill out onto the streets, it can be a prelude to a change from dictatorship to democracy.

There are times in life when the Underground Pit is closer to the surface naturally, as in adolescence when crossing that bridge from the Right Side of the New Brain to the Left, and also in midlife when the need for the Underground Pit to clear out some of the store and complete unfinished business becomes critical. The next chapter will look at these two critical periods in human development and their role in Integrated Thinking.

4 THE CROSSING BRIDGE

Every element of the whole human system, every emotion, every part of the brain, is essential to human development, and the aim is to develop them in stages at the appropriate time and in the appropriate way, and then integrate them into a bigger framework.

Built into the overall programme of human development are two stages when the Crossing Bridge, the *corpus callosum* at the central crossroads in the brain, can be said to play an essential role in this inner integration. The two stages are adolescence and midlife, when the brain is rewired - particularly the Forebrain - by breaking old connections and making new ones, so that disintegration contributes to greater integration. These key crossover times can be very difficult to navigate, and there is always the temptation to turn back towards old familiar ways. The role of 'I', the ego, is critical to both stages.

EGO

Adolescents cross the bridge from the Right Side to the Left Side of the New Brain, which has the dominant responsibility for the next stage of development when young people move into the 'real world' outside the family circle. The ego plays an important role at this stage as the basis of a person's unique individuality, able to deal with the realities and challenges of life with resourcefulness, initiative and confidence. Initially, as with any stage of development, the ego tests the boundaries, makes mistakes and learns from them to become more skilled at using its abilities.

Yet, like the unconscious, it can be portrayed as negative but this is usually when an unrestrained ego exceeds its boundaries to become no longer the 'I' of individuality and independence, but an egotistical Mighty I, the brain's sole superpower, in control of everything and everyone, but actually detached from reality.

"When we are in the 'I' state, our empathy is switched off and we relate only to things, or to people as if they were just things", is how Simon Baron-Cohen describes it in *Zero Degrees of Empathy*. And like a tyrant when threatened, the Mighty I will use all its weapons of aggression, self-justification and denial to remain in power, crushing resistance, draining resources, misusing energy supplies and turning a blind eye to law and morality.

The ego, or awareness of individual independence, is associated with free will and with the right to choose one's own path. It should include taking responsibility for the consequences of those choices and actions, and this activates the Forebrain and its moral decision-making, so free will is not like the so-called 'free market' or 'free press', untrammelled by regulations.

What exactly is 'free will' has been debated for centuries, but an image here might be more useful that a closely argued debate. I like to link the idea of human willpower to the image of horsepower. Both our wills and horses can be allowed to run wild, or they can be as stubborn as mules, or they can be well trained and disciplined over a period of time, their energy harnessed and used for our benefit in self-control.

If the latter, then the ego or 'I' of young adulthood can use all that greatly increased willpower or horsepower to give it the freedom of the road - to refer back to an earlier image of the different parts of the brain being like the gears in a car. However, if the will has been allowed to run wild, and the young person has not learnt to adapt to society's rules, it would be like letting someone onto the roads in a car without first passing their driving test.

Willpower, the keystone of individual identity, first makes its presence known in the 'terrible two's', the beginning of a long period of training needed to harness willpower for the benefit of the person and society. The Gut Brain, the unconscious and the Primal Brain have been in control until this stage, but it is at about two years old that the Gut Brain needs finally to let go control. Toilet training during the period of copying and co-operation immediately before the 'terrible two's' is how the Gut Brain learns that the head brain is taking over, but if the child is given free will in how and when he is toilet trained, then the Gut Brain, understandably, believes it is still in charge.

The 'terrible two's' is when a toddler tries out his first solo venture into the Left Side of personal choice as he realises that it's not only his parents who can say no: he can too. He doesn't have to do what his god-like parents want him to! As the unrealistic mini-ego tests out the extent of its power, his parents have to use their more developed Left Side to draw boundary lines for him, in order to re-direct that energy back into the socialising Right Side of the New Brain.

Using the imagery of horsepower again, this would be the stage when a horse is first brought into a contained space and its raw power harnessed into a co-operative partnership with its rider. In former days, its will would be broken (which still happens to children in some places), now it is a more gentle approach - but still the horse and the child's Gut and Primal Brains have to accept restrictions on their freedom.

As a baby, he thought he was all-important, now he has to accept that he is not master of all he surveys, the centre of universal attention, and that he has to learn to share and let others have a turn. It must seem as devastating as when people realised the earth was not the centre of the universe, but just one planet revolving around the sun in a small galaxy amongst millions. Some even in adulthood still refuse to accept this personal demotion from being the centre of the universe to being just one amongst many.

ADOLESCENCE

A child has to have clear boundary lines established for him within the family and learn the rules during the socialising stage of development, just as he needs to understand the lines between the pavement and the road. Steven Pinker in *The Better Angels Of Our Nature* identifies the social rules as derived from a few principles, such as, "Control your appetites, delay gratification, consider the sensibilities of others, distance yourself from your animal natures". In other words, the role of the Primal Brain has to give way as the New Brain and Forebrain develop. In adolescence, the developing ego, with its willpower driving it forward, leads a teenager away from the security of the family to face the challenges of the outside world.

However, according to Deepak Chopra in *Superbrain*, "Human beings are the only creatures who do not mature automatically. The world is full of people stuck in childhood or adolescence, no matter how old they happen to be. No project is more decisive for personal power and happiness than the project of becoming a mature adult".

There seems to be something about today's world that makes it more likely than in previous generations for a person to stay a kidult or in transition, stuck on the Crossing Bridge and never making it across to full independence. Stories of heroes and heroines can help young people make this crossing, rather than the look-at-me behaviour of attention-seeking celebrities.

Stages

Young people need a firm foundation before launching off on their own, if only as something to kick against. At this crossroads in life, the pressure is immense. Young people feel the push to leave the family and group dependency, but swing back to the familiar when it all seems too much. Below is the fiery sexual furnace rearing up from the Primal Brain, determined to fulfil its role in creating the next generation. There is a waterfall from the Forebrain above, flowing with ideas, ideals and dreams. Some get lost in its fantasy world while others retreat into earlier stages of human social development, such as tribal allegiance.

Adolescents are trying to separate their Emotional Wheel from the larger family Wheel to create their own physical and individual psychological space. They need clearly marked staging posts on this crossing, not the sometimes brutal initiation ceremonies of old, but markers like earning pocket money, proms at leaving school, driving a car, a gap year. It is hard work being a teenager, and there are all those physical changes to adapt to, they have life-changing exams and have to decide who they want to be and what career they want to follow.

Adolescence is when teenagers play with roles, and 'who will I be today?' feeds a whole industry of changing fashions by designers using pubescent models. Because the adolescent ego is still developing, it has not yet had its boundaries defined by bumping up against reality, and so can 'think it knows it all' and take unreasonable risks. It is the same with any skill, for example like a toddler learning to walk; he bumps into furniture and does not see the dangers around him. Only when the Forebrain gets its act together in their late teens or early twenties will a young person be more reliably able to foresee the consequences of their actions, and their effect on others.

Pruning

David Bainbridge in his book *Teenagers* gives a vivid description of the drastic pruning that happens in the brain during adolescence. "Throughout teenage years, the overgrown brambles of the childhood cortex are savagely hewn to leave a beautifully minimalist arboreal structure. The [Forebrain] is subject to even greater attrition and it has been suggested that this leads to increased analytical abilities as well as the more disruptive aspects of the teenage [brain] - lack of foresight, emotional volatility, impulsiveness and lack of thought for others".

This pruning leaves a lot of debris to be cleared up. Teenagers are known for creating a holy mess, reflecting the messiness of their internal world. "The bomb site that is a teenager's room could well be mirroring their life and their brain", thinks Nicola Morgan in *Blame My Brain*. Teenagers show their independence by breaking some of the family or social rules, and by having their own way of dressing, communicating and thinking.

Different Levels

It is quite possible to cross the bridge mentally and leave emotional development behind, or vice versa, so that the two functions of the brain operate at different levels. When information-processing is more advanced, with a focus on facts, figures and 'things', emotional maturity may be lagging behind. One example might be the boss at work who becomes a baby at home, unable to fend for herself; or someone who controls numbers in the outside world but loses all control emotionally in a personal relationship when faced with frustration, like a toddler having a temper tantrum.

On the other hand, when emotional development is stronger, with a focus on personal and social skills and relationships, then detachment and analysis can be less developed, so they take everything very personally and emotionally rather than seeing situations objectively.

It may take some time before the two functions are re-integrated. However, if a teenager does not make it across that bridge emotionally, he can remain attached to the group, dependent on someone bigger or stronger than himself, such as a gang leader or a more powerful personality, or attaches himself to a cult or ideology that offers a bigger vision - or just a life of dependency on social welfare,

Without the active, initiating drive of the Left Side, there can be a tendency to slip back into passive self-pity, even take on the role of victim or martyr. Of course, there are real victims and they should be encouraged to speak out, to be believed and supported.

Role of Adults

Teenagers' loyalty or attachment moves from the family to their friends, usually of the same gender, who support each other during this crossover period. In previous generations and in many parts of the world today, boys and girls copied their parents rather than create individual identities, but parents in the West these days have different roles to play. To gain independence, girls may have to reject their mother or her ways, while boys have a need to overthrow their father, psychologically if not physically (although beating a father at sport will do it!). Both boys and girls need a strong figure, usually of their own gender, as mentor or idol on the other side of the bridge encouraging them to cross.

Strong female role models who have succeeded through ability not appearance whom girls can copy are very recent in today's society, while it is difficult for a boy to complete this critical developmental task if his father is absent or is himself part of a dependency culture. A gang leader can fill the gap for some with a regression to dangerous initiations. For Damian Barr in *Maggie And Me*, however, it was Margaret Thatcher, his 'other mother,' who showed him the way by making "a hero of the individual".

To break away from all that is familiar is painful but the surge of sex hormones in the Primal Brain helps. Maybe those social restrictions on adolescent sexual activity had a useful purpose in the past, encouraging teenagers to leave the family home and set up their own home base with a partner, as well as ensuring parenthood came with a greater understanding of its responsibilities. Certainly the development of the Left Side's critical faculties and the Forebrain's idealism play their part, with the criticism directed at parents, systems and sometimes their own physical appearance, as well as school texts. Idealistic young people challenge Authority with a capital A, often condemning a distant 'them' for their problems rather than blaming those closest to them especially if they are still dependent on them. Some continue this attitude well beyond adolescence.

Individualism for All?

The independent stage of development first evolved in the West. In *Letters To Lily* Alan Macfarlane points out that, "Two hundred years ago, there was nowhere on earth where you could have been an individual who could act on your own, have your own rights, practice any religion, vote for any party, do the job you were qualified for, marry whom you want, keep the money you earn. Individualism, a location of economic, religious, political and social power in the hands of each person, emerged suddenly and dramatically". These rights were restricted to men until the 20th century.

Many non-Western societies still do not allow a young person to become independent, to criticise their elders, develop their own sense of identity, choose their own partner or even their own clothes. It is particularly difficult for young people from immigrant families with a stronger sense of family or group identity, who are brought up in the West, surrounded by a world that arouses parts of them which their upbringing does not allow them to express, but which more powerful male leaders can misuse.

MIDLIFE

Crossing the bridge at the brain's crossroads is a central feature of midlife as well as adolescence. It is also when the brain is again restructured, with a particular focus on the Forebrain, and when the ego plays another key role. However, although there are some similarities, such as 'senior moments' and teenage inattention both indicating that the Forebrain is being pruned, there are also major differences between the two periods of change as midlife is a more mature stage of development.

Two Way

Crossing the bridge is an image, you will recall, that refers to the handover in balance between the Right and Left Sides of the New Brain. In adolescence, teenagers pass over the Crossing Bridge mainly from Right Side to Left, when the full range of human potential has been shaped into a unique individual by emphasising certain aspects and minimising others. Midlife, by contrast, offers the opportunity to explore and re-integrate those underused or missing aspects and stages of development, and the Crossing Bridge is also far more two-way.

In the traditional midlife pattern, men and women used to cross over in opposite directions, with men developing their Right Side of the New Brain skills, while women crossed over from Right to Left, to develop a stronger sense of their own identity and more confidence in their role in the outside world. Recent personal, social and political changes have affected this pattern for some, and these changes will be explored more in Section 2.

Although men and women in the traditional pattern were crossing the bridge in the opposite direction in midlife, they had the same purpose, and that was to develop all parts of the brain and create a balance between information-processing and emotional maturity. Men have been described as channelling the aggressiveness of their youth into more peace-keeping roles, becoming more interested in social connections, while women become more active in the world outside the family and broaden their scope of involvement to include management and leadership roles.

Developmental Intelligence

As with adolescents, the physical, psychological, emotional and mental changes in midlife are accompanied by changes in the Forebrain. The re-wiring in adolescence is to prepare young people for life in the world beyond the family circle; whereas in midlife, this re-wiring is to prepare older people for a different kind of thinking. In his book *The Mature Mind*, Gene Cohen defines this as, "The maturing of cognition, emotional intelligence, judgement, social skills, life experience and consciousness, and their integration. Developmental Intelligence does not kick in fully until midlife. It is the basis of wisdom".

Midlife is another critical time for the ego, but unlike in adolescence when it is just beginning to spread its wings, the ego in midlife has to do the last thing it wants to do - it has to let go control, as part of the maturing process. That can feel like losing everything you have worked for, and that is hard at any stage of life, but for an overblown, overgrown ego, the Mighty I, it can feel like defeat or even death. Some psychologists have compared the Mighty I to a dictator, suppressing information and re-writing history in the service of preserving an all-powerful self-image and its position of power, refusing to step down from the stage. The devastation this can cause is clearly seen in the outside world, but it happens within too.

As we have seen, handing over primary control from one stage of development to the next is rarely a smooth handover of power. The next stage of development for the ego is not death, but moving from a dominant role to playing a supporting role in the greater integration of human potential, what Jung called the birth of the True Self. Psychologist Abraham Maslow described this process as Self-actualisation, and it is what makes the midlife stage so critical to human development - although there are some overblown egos that never adapt to the change and would prefer death to playing second fiddle.

Another difference between midlife and adolescence is that in youth, there seems to be all the time in the world to achieve one's ambitions, whereas in midlife, the opposite is true. Time seems mysteriously to speed up, and the amount of time left to pass on experiences and knowledge is shrinking. Gail Sheey in her book on midlife, *Passages*, calls this the 'deadline decade'. There is a sense of urgency and a desire to get things done, a resurgence of the dreams and ideals of youth, but this time with the experience to know what works and what doesn't. The unconscious has its own role to play, bringing to the surface uncompleted developmental tasks from the past, all part of the drive towards inner integration.

Bodies change in midlife, so do hormone levels, and also the grey matter inside our brains. Grey matter, which processes information, is reduced while white matter that connects different parts of the brain actually increases, encouraging the maturing process of Developmental Intelligence, as Gene Cohen called it.

There is more white matter naturally in women's brains, and scientists have discovered that male brains in midlife develop a more 'female' pattern of greater connectivity between the two Sides of the New Brain, and so can see the bigger picture when making decisions. "All these adaptations reduce the amount of energy required to perform tasks, and middle aged humans are very energy-efficient", comments Mona Lisa Schultz in *The New Feminine Brain*.

Critical to the integration of these changes at midlife is the Crossing Bridge at the brain's central crossroads, whose integrating role has been enhanced and made more efficient by this increase in white matter.

BRIDGE OR WALL

Instead of an open Crossing Bridge, however, there seems to be a border control or even a wall in many people, separating Left and Right Sides of the New Brain, just as the Berlin Wall separated West and East Germany in the Cold War, or like the wall on the left bank in Israel increases tension and conflict, making integration more difficult. The wall can divide North and South too, separating the Forebrain's ideas and vision from the Primal Brain's application of practical reality.

Turning a Blind Eye

Conflict between different parts of the brain is called 'cognitive dissonance' or emotional and mental discord. It is at the Crossing Bridge or *corpus callosum*, which translates as Wounded Body, where the pain of this discord is felt. To resolve those differences and continue to keep that Crossing Bridge open is hard work.

A strategy to avoid that work is called wilful blindness in law or *anosognosia* in neuroscience, or more simply, neglect. Rita Carter in *Mapping the Mind* describes people with neglect as being blind to half the world, or 'turning a blind eye'. This can be positive, as when switching off visual fields temporarily allows new insights to flash onto the mind's eye, as the brain makes use at the same time of the Right Side's greater connectivity over a wider field than the straight and short Left Side field of operation.

In neglect's negative role, however, differences between what we say and what we do, between the image we have of ourselves and our actual behaviour, are habitually denied and hidden behind internal defensive walls, and our mental constructs become increasingly out of sync with reality. For example, I may have an image of myself as a caring person, but if I literally turn a blind eye and walk away from an elderly man who has fallen in the street, then there is an internal conflict between my image and the reality of my actions. If I acknowledge and regret my failure to act, then I have not neglected the opportunity to learn from my mistakes, and if possible, take steps to help later. Or I may deny there is a problem and let my internal spin-doctor resolve the conflict for me by saying, "Someone else was there to look after him". Then another brick goes in the wall and the integrating role of the Crossing Bridge is made more difficult.

Building Walls

It is not just behaviour that builds walls. Differences between ideas and contradictory facts can also be denied, so we neglect to update our mental constructs. We all do it, and the more rigid our mental constructs or ways of thinking, the more we neglect to adjust them to facts that do not fit the theories. To overcome wilful blindness, we need to make greater use of our Forebrain's moral courage, sense of responsibility and justice, and its ability to see the whole picture and take the long-term view.

Defences erected during childhood, however, are the cause of some forms of blindness. These are not wilful, but were necessary for survival so that a terrified child could hide behind them, and they can be the most difficult to recognise and change. We all 'wall' off things we do not want to admit to, just as men used to refuse to admit women to public life, decision-making, business or clubs; in some societies, women are literally hidden behind walls. These are walls usually erected by men, perhaps reflecting their own inner walls, denying and neglecting their own 'feminine' side.

Bennett and Sally Shaywitz' experiments at Yale University, reported in *The Guardian*, 5 August 1995, showed that men were more likely to have an inner wall than women, due to biological and social reasons, which could include the tendency in men for the Left Side of the New Brain to dominate with its emphasis on division and compartments.

Beginning during the foetal stage, the female brain is different from the male and now that women have taken advantage of an education system devised by men (therefore with a Left Side bias), women's brains are developing in very different ways to previous generations of women or men, according to Mona Lisa Schultz. While in *The End Of Men*, Hannah Rosin explores the ways in which men have fallen behind the recent rapid changes in women's brains and lives.

When there is a wall between the two Sides of the New Brain, or even just restricted exchange, we have to go down into the Primal Brain to reconnect the two Sides through an earlier crossing called the *anterior commissure*, in what Rita Carter calls "the cerebral underworld". Entering this psychological tunnel is a well-documented aspect of the midlife crisis, watched over in mythology by Hermes, the shape-changer who looks both ways. It is in the dark of the Underground Pit that we come face to face with the missing, neglected, rejected or overused parts of ourselves in order to integrate them into the whole picture of the True Self.

Yet going back into the Primal Brain can also feel like revisiting one's earlier life, particularly the other key stage of adolescence, so perhaps that is why many in midlife seem determined to recapture their youth or act out sexual fantasies with the powerful motor(bike) that throbs between their legs! Or more down to earth, by returning to higher education interrupted or not completed earlier in life.

Returning to an earlier stage of life makes sense if it is a phase in the overall integration process - *"reculer pour mieux sauter"* is how the French describe this pulling back to better leap forward - or it can be to regain a sense of fun and adventure that can get lost in a life of adult and family responsibilities. Problems occur when we get stuck at this younger stage of development, reluctant to move on and mature integration is postponed.

SECTION REVIEW

In this Section, we have seen how all the four main parts of the human brain, linked through the Crossing Bridge, make their contribution to the different stages of human development. In Chapter 1, we considered the information-processing function and then integrated it with emotional development in Chapter 2. Next we explored the role of the unconscious, and in Chapter 4 we looked at the critical crossover times during adolescence and midlife.

It is clear that many things can affect development at any stage, and that seemingly small omissions or actions can have long-lasting consequences, which makes raising children the most daunting task. There is a great deal of knowledge that could be more widely available to those who need it most, potential and actual parents and other carers.

The aim of this Section was to see if we could clarify what is 'our way of thinking' that people are saying needs to change. Acknowledging a need for change does not mean that what has gone before has been wrong, rather that it may no longer be the most appropriate way of thinking for the next stage of development.

From this brief overview of how the brain works, it seems that rather than just one way of thinking, there are many different ways, depending on which part of the brain is more dominant, whether that is the Primal Brain of sport, escapism, eating and sex (the Four F's), or the communal Right Side, the compartmentalising Left Side or the reflective, mature Forebrain - or even the unconscious and Gut Brain. If we miss out or neglect any stage of information-processing or emotional development, our brains are unbalanced and so is our thinking.

The question of what is in control of our thinking depends on the stage of development we have reached. These many ways of thinking are often contradictory, conflicted and confusing, and this is reflected in the societies the brain creates.

The New IT seeks to rebalance these differences, and to integrate them into a bigger picture of human development that is appropriate for today's time and place. Deepak Chopra claims that, "The best way to achieve health, happiness and success is by balancing all four phases of the brain. Your brain goes out of balance when you favour one part over another. It is easy to identify with one phase of the brain, which encourages it to dominate."

In Section 2, we will take Integrated Thinking a step further by showing how the framework for the inner world of human development can be integrated with the world outside, by exploring how the brain seems to use its own workings as a template for the social and political systems and structures it creates, with particular reference to Britain in the early 21st century.

SECTION 2

SOCIAL AND POLITICAL DEVELOPMENT

"Your brain creates your world. Everything begins and ends with your brain".
Daniel Amen

INTRODUCTION

In Section 1 we saw that our 'present way of thinking' is in fact made up of many ways, related to different stages of brain development. Integrating these differences will reduce inner conflict, people can respond in the most appropriate way to changing circumstances and make best use of their inner resources so that more evolved stages of brain development play a greater role in their thinking. This new way of thinking will create a corresponding change in the outside world, for in Deepak Chopra's view in *Superbrain*, "The physical world we experience only mirrors our human nervous system".

In Section 2, we will be looking at why we would want to change the way society works, where those changes might be, and how that might be done. I am proposing that one way in which society could change would be through using the model of Integrated Thinking, the New IT, based on how the brain works. In doing this, we would simply be following the brain's example of linking inside and out, as the brain seems to use its internal structures and systems as a template or model for the systems and structures it creates in the outside world.

As with personal development, Integrated Thinking could create a framework for social development that integrates differences which presently cause social conflict; it could help society respond to new challenges more appropriately, and where some of the systems that reflect or evoke earlier stages of development have come to dominate in society, it could support better use of more evolved parts of the brain.

If we do find that the social and political worlds are a projection of the internal workings of the brain, this offers two opportunities for change. If we change the way our brains work, we can change the social and political worlds they create; while if we change society, our brains respond accordingly. Some of these changes are already happening.

Chapter 5 begins the exploration of integrating personal and social development by looking at how the different parts of the brain are reflected in British society today, and Chapter 6 looks at how the same model could be applied to political development. Chapter 7 reviews the similarities between the unconscious and the criminal underworld, and in Chapter 8 we look at what anti-social behaviour tells us about the society our brains have created.

5 SOCIAL DEVELOPMENT

The social systems and constructs that our brains have created reflect the differing ways of thinking associated with the different parts of the brain, as outlined in Section 1. In this Chapter, we will look at some of the many ways in which the internal workings of the Primal Brain, the two Sides of the New Brain and the Forebrain (see Figure 1) are reflected in British society today.

SURVIVAL

We saw in Chapter 1 that the Primal Brain has many roles, but that survival remains its prime focus. Death rates have been decreasing over the last century in most of the developed world, but the role of the Primal Brain has not decreased to the same degree: in fact, some would say its role has come to dominate many areas of social life. We will examine its social significance by looking at three of its key functions: automatic programming, the Four F's of fight, flight, food and the final f, and the Emotional Wheel.

Automatic Programming

We have seen how the autopilot of the Primal Brain, the Serpent, takes over skills and tasks once they become automatic, so that people can use their more evolved brains in order to learn something new and progress. At least, that is the theory, rather like the theory that machines and computers would give people more time for other activities, when in reality both the autopilot and computers seem to be taking over more and more of people's lives.

The autopilot is the brain's default mode, and takes over when people are tired or stressed. Because of the long working hours, information overload and demands of society today, many people feel they are operating on auto. Some would go further and say that life today is leading to the creation of an isolated 'autistic' society (Yehuda Baruch, 1997, *Journal of General Management*).

Some aspects of autism, such as prodigious copying and memory skills, might indicate human potential unaffected by pruning, but Simon Baron-Cohen in *Zero Degrees of Empathy* describes autism as the 'extreme male brain'. I understand this to mean that characteristics often associated with the Left Side of New Brain and masculine thinking - such as personal detachment, less empathy and greater systemising skills - have been taken to the extreme in autism. It is men's brains that have created the world's systems, structures and societies, so it is to be expected that they reflect men's thinking. But how does that kind of thinking become extreme in a social environment?

In her book, *The Moral State We're In*, Julia Neuberger highlights the risks of a range of institutional behaviours to the most vulnerable in our society. If these behaviours were applied to individuals, one could refer to them as being symptoms of 'on the spectrum' autism. They include the fear of risk, change and strangers; the need for detailed rules; the lack of physical contact and personal interactions, and the lack of compassion.

It is now believed that those with autism have fewer mirror cells in their brains, so that their brains build mental constructs that do not include the emotions of others, or sometimes even exclude other people themselves. Internet social networking such as Facebook also reduces input to and from the socialising Right Side of the New Brain because of its lack of physical contact and personal interactions, but activates the Primal Brain's autopilot and the Left Side's detachment. This could contribute to the sense of being part of an 'autistic society'.

How has the Primal Brain's autopilot come to play such a strong role in society? The increasing automation of many activities, such as production lines or computers, while working in a competitive environment in a consumer society, have been accompanied by an overemphasis on personal choice beginning in very early childhood.

This could have created what might be described as a 'rat run' superhighway between the Gut Brain, the Serpent of the Primal Brain and the Left Side of the New Brain, which in extreme cases can virtually bypass the Right Side, with its concern for other members of the group, and also sideline the Forebrain of creativity and morality in favour of being 'online'. This kind of thinking has become very dominant in some areas of British society today.

Four F's

Karen Armstrong refers to the Four F's in *Twelve Steps to a Compassionate Life*. "Selfish egotism is rooted in the 'old brain' which was bequeathed to us by the reptiles that struggled out of the primal slime 500m years ago. Wholly intent on personal survival, these creatures were motivated by mechanisms that neuroscientists have called the Four F's: Fighting, Fleeing, Feeding and .... Reproduction."

I will look at each of these activities in turn, and how they affect modern society.

Fight:

One aspect of fighting or aggression is hunting. The world of the Serpent or *reptilian core* is the predatory jungle, when Man the Hunter dominated. Man no longer needed to hunt once cattle and sheep were farmed and meat was freely available, but somehow that powerful image survived and is still used to explain certain behaviours - with good reason. This primitive part of the brain is automatically aroused when making a killing on the stock market in the concrete jungle, or when sexual predators stalk their prey in cold blood through urban streets, looking for 'fresh meat', or in the feeding frenzy by the media when a politician is brought down.

Flight:

Running away from danger is one of the body's essential survival mechanisms, but in social terms, flight can also be a running away from reality or responsibility, escaping into a world of fantasy. There is a reward system in the brain that gives a buzz of pleasure chemicals when we engage in novel experiences or exciting activities. Feedback in the form of habituation ensures that after sufficient repetitions, the sensation becomes commonplace and the buzz level drops so we then move onto something that gives us a new buzz and we move forward rather than stay stuck on one thing.

If there is a problem with the feedback mechanism, then the brain can get stuck or frozen on the same activity, but needs more and more stimulation to receive the same level of reward buzz. This brain malfunction is reflected in the outside world in the form of social malfunctioning, for example in the abuse of the four F's, or in the abuse of drugs or Internet games, creating a fantasy world as a flight from reality and its consequences.

Food:

The brain, and in particular the Forebrain, takes up more energy in the form of glucose than any other organ in the body, and different stages of brain development have different requirements. For example, breast milk helps make the myelin sheaths that protect a baby's new brain connections, like insulation around electrical wiring.

Is it possible that the milk, orange juice and cod liver oil (all providing key brain nutrients) which were given for free to children after World War II had some connection with the later social and cultural explosion of the 60's? Today's junk food, with its adulterated oils and sugar derivatives, feeds the bad bacteria in our guts and behaviour associated with the Gut Brain. While according to Steve Jones in *The Serpent's Promise*, antibiotics given to animals increased the rate they put on weight, but eating their meat can also affect consumers' appetite mechanism. This can have effects on an individual's health and the National Health Service.

The right nutrition can also have a beneficial effect in improving behaviour, as has been shown with prisoners. In *The Better Angels Of Our Nature*, Steven Pinker refers to a study reported in *Science* in 2009 that, "Several placebo-controlled studies have suggested that providing prisoners with dietary supplements can reduce their rate of impulsive violence". Eating the right brain food is important for us all. John Arden in *Rewire Your Brain* gives helpful advice about the kind of diet and exercises our brains need, especially if we are to change and improve the way they work.

Final F:

As far as arousal is concerned, size really does count after all. The area of men's brains devoted to sex is much bigger than women's. "Men have double the brain space and processing power devoted to sex as females. Just as women have an 8-lane superhighway for processing emotion while men have a small country road, men have a major airport hub for processing thoughts about sex, where women have a small, private airfield", explains Louann Brizendine in *The Female Brain*. And to keep it big, everything has to be 'sexy' or 'hot' today, even boring documents.

Caitlin Moran in *The Times* on 26 June 2006 gave a woman's perspective. "I was struck by how incredibly useless looking sexy is. Practically speaking, the only time that a woman need concern herself with looking sexy is about 20 minutes before she has sex." Yet much of today's society seems devoted to increasing the amount of brain space devoted to arousal, particularly in men.

The artificially swollen 'bee-sting' lips of female sexual arousal, the surgically enhanced breasts just like mummy's when breastfeeding and the changing erogenous zones of fashion to stop men's brains habituating, all make sure men get the message. As Jeremy Clarkson wrote in the *Sunday Times* on 23 September 2012, "How can breasts be a big deal when half the world has them? Well I'll tell you how. Because the other half can't really ever think of anything else". Or is he only speaking of men like himself?

61

Keeping men feeling sexy can make women feel safe and wanted, but not always. Sexual arousal has changed with the freely available pornography on the Internet, linking sex more with violence than with love. The Primal Brain is not the cleverest cookie in the tin, and it can get sex and aggression mixed up in rape and war. Margaret Cook in *Lords of Creation* tells how, "Waiting with their heads down during the frenzy of artillery bombardment to go into an offensive, many men have experienced sexual hallucinations, often violent, explicit and obscene, provoking arousal to the point of ejaculation." Anger can be justified, war sometimes even necessary, but rape can never be necessary or justified.

The link between sexual arousal and aggression can be useful to sports coaches who show erotic films before rugby matches to improve performances (see Scott Drawer's 2012 study in *Hormones and Behaviour*), or by those in the financial markets. John Naish in *The Times*, 12 April 2008, reported that, "Research by Knutson on male brain scans showed that erotic images and risky financial decisions boost activity in the same area of the brain, and that the stimuli reinforce each other. The link may be due to the fact that risk-taking, possession-grabbing and sexual conquest could all be linked to our ancient evolutionary brains". Society seems to encourage the primitive link between sexual arousal, aggression and risk-taking (which includes over-spending) with big bonuses and sexy images to sell consumer goods, but would it not be better to discourage it?

The Four F's could also be called the Four C's of Conflict, Competition, Consumption and Compulsions, which is often how modern Western life is portrayed in the media, reflecting the dominance of this primitive part of the brain. It is hard to avoid the conclusion that the Primal Brain continues to play a major role in society today, and its activities are not always well regulated by mature Forebrains (or regulatory bodies), even though the Primal Brain's prime role in ensuring survival has largely been met.

Emotional Wheel

Now we turn to the Emotional Wheel, inherited from warm-blooded mammals, and consider its role in ensuring the care of the young, the old and the sick, the very corner stone of a caring society - although these areas seem to be disproportionately affected by recent economic cuts.

Before birth, a baby is attached to his mother's placenta by a lifeline, the umbilical cord from his gut. She feeds him with what he needs and takes away waste through her blood. During birth, her body and his are flooded with the chemical oxytocin, giving them a natural high to alleviate the pain of birth and to trigger the compassion that comes after the grief of labour. Compassion completes the circuit of the Emotional Wheel, and ensures the survival of the human race through human bonding.

Michel Odent in *The Scientification of Love* sees oxytocin as the hormone of love. "It is involved in labour, lactation and during intercourse". Breastfeeding continues the release of oxytocin, making it pleasurable for both mother and child, and helps open up their two Emotional Wheels to create a single emotional system. But oxytocin is not for women only as it can also be stimulated in men when they care for the young and vulnerable.

The same chemicals are released later when people fall in love, make love or trust someone; it has been called the cuddling or commitment hormone. It would seem to make sense to know one's partner is trustworthy before having sex, or else the trust response may be inappropriately activated.

Oxytocin is not only important in creating personal bonds, however; it also has a critical role in social development. "Oxytocin is the 'social glue' that binds families, communities and societies together", was Paul Zak's view in *The Observer* 21 August 2011. Yet if the attachment created by compassion between mother and baby does not happen at the right time or in the right way, or is broken too soon, the need to attach or 'hook up' does not go away: it is too vital for survival.

"If as a baby you didn't have a strong attachment with your mother, then you feel insecure. You spend your life looking for something else to hold onto. That's the core of an addictive personality", Seth Freedman states in his book *Binge Trading*. Sometimes the hook attaches itself to a substitute, such as the mother church, alma mater, Queen and country, the motherland, the 'mother of all Parliaments', or liberty, justice or truth with their female statues, or just to a partner who takes on the role of 'mother'.

This attachment hook can wait in the dark for a long time until it can spring into action, perhaps triggered by the psychological stroking that being the centre of public and media attention can offer. But when hooked up in this way, those on the receiving end need to be constantly fed, like babies hooked up to their mothers, and without constant reassurance, they can feel as vulnerable as a baby.

Sometimes compassion, the emotional connection linked to attachment, can be twisted in the unconscious into obsessions for people or things, including fetishes for shoes, rubber or being beaten. In South Korea, some children are being treated for computer addiction. Yet the Emotional Wheel tries to complete its circuit somehow, even though the new 'lifeline' can hold back progress personally or socially.

BOTH SIDES NOW

We now move onto the New Brain to see how it is reflected in social development. The ways of thinking associated with the two Sides of the New Brain, Right and Left with their different emphasis on the group or the individual, are reflected in many aspects of the social systems and structures that the human brain has created. These two ways of thinking are also called E-type thinking focusing on empathy, and S-type thinking, or systemising thought.

Sue Palmer in *21st Century Boys* believes that civil society depends on E-type thinking or empathy, which is more developed in girls and women, while the ability to systemise underpins our capacity for rational thought. The capacity to build tools and technology, models and machines, empires and economies are based on the principles of systemising-type thought, or S-type, in which many men excel. However, as Sue Palmer also points out, when the drive for systems, status and success is allowed to accelerate without the counterbalance of empathy, it can threaten the survival of the species. Integrated Thinking seeks to address the risk this poses for society today by rebalancing the two ways of thinking and by developing a bigger framework.

Each Side's way of thinking has its advantages and disadvantages. Those who rely more on the Left Side can find it hard to think 'outside the box', while those in whom the Right Side is dominant can go round and round in circles without coming to a decision. This is why it is best if they work together. However, Western society tends to emphasise Left Side values, such as individual achievement and standing on one's own two feet, as typified by the goal scorer, captains of industry or the entrepreneur.

The Left-Side emphasis on personal choice is appropriate for adults after they have developed their Right Side, but many Western societies encourage it at every stage of development, so that even very young children are allowed to choose everything - what they eat, do, wear or when to be toilet-trained. Although no-one wants to return to the old days of children being seen but not heard, this overemphasis on personal choice at such a young age strengthens the rat-run between the Gut Brain, the Primal Brain and Left Side of the New Brain I described earlier, and reduces the role of the adaptive Right Side of the New Brain that develops social and civil behaviour.

We will now take a brief look at how the differences between the two Sides are reflected in the systems and structures in the outside world, using examples from agriculture, transport, community groups, business and education, and also consider how the brain itself tries to fill a gap between the two Sides.

Agriculture

We saw earlier how the Right Side of the New Brain favours circles, connections and relationships and tends to be stronger in women and communities.

In earlier days of agriculture, this way of thinking was reflected in the way the farming community grew diverse crops as part of an interconnected system, planted according to cycles and seasons, bringing benefit to other plants and the soil. Both the land and animals were husbanded, and houses in villages too were often built in a circle. This kind of agriculture is still practised in many developing parts of the world today, and recently similar principles have been re-introduced into the West, for example in *Creating a Forest Garden* by Martin Crawford.

On the other hand, the Left Side favours lines, divisions, facts and figures, and taking things apart. Today large-scale agri-businesses are based on Left Side thinking with one crop grown in straight lines, cities are rectilinear, and even animal welfare is automated as part of a production line. Organic farming seeks to reverse this trend.

Transport

Transport also reflects the difference between the two Sides. Compare investment in group travel like the railways in a more family- or a group-oriented society such as Germany, with investment in individual car travel in the predominantly Left Side thinking USA - or in the UK, where we even drive on the left side. Co-incidence probably!

Community Groups and Business

The Right Side of the New Brain, however, is strongly indicated in many community groups that focus on connections, circles, networks, relationships and communication, all vital for strengthening group cohesion. Sometimes the circle can become closed, so that someone who says or does something different from the consensus is seen as a threat to group security, and can be excluded.

On the other hand, working in business helps develop Left Side objectivity, project and financial management skills, by encouraging initiative, self-responsibility and leadership, with a focus on delivery not group discussion.

These differences between the two sides are reflected in the language they use. As Rt Rev James Jones, Bishop of Liverpool, pointed out on his website, "Communities tend to use organic language, such as 'seeds, planting, renewal', while those who control the money tend to use mechanical language such as 'triggers, buttons, levers and targets'." An understanding of the other side's point of view, use of language and skills is part of the integrating process.

Many community activists resist adopting skills that they associate with business because 'Big Business' is seen as a major cause of today's environmental and economic crises. But by working together, both community groups and business can learn from each other. Integrated Thinking also means that people at all levels of management need to be emotionally and intellectually balanced, so that this - and a greater use of the Forebrain's moral awareness - is reflected in their decision-making.

The key point is that we are all, as individuals, communities and nations, at different stages of development so that one size does not fit all. For example, while many in the West, with its over-emphasis on individualism, would benefit from greater community involvement, that would not apply to those who had not yet crossed the bridge from group dependency to independence.

These would include over-idealistic activists, some small town communities, children from immigrant families, most of the developing nations and countries involved in the Arab Revolution. The latter are seeking greater individualism and self-determination to help break away from the dominance of group conformity. Yet, although one size or solution does not fit all, they can all fit within the framework of the New IT, Integrated Thinking and a greater use of the Crossing Bridge between the two Sides.

Education

In education too, one size does not fit all. Barbara Arrowsmith-Young in *The Woman Who Changed Her Brain* defines, "A learning dysfunction as an area of the brain that is weaker than other areas in a network. If stimulation placed more demands on that region of the brain than another, then change would occur in the targeted part of the brain, and that would have an effect on the whole network". She recommends that every child be assessed at an early age, so that their brain deficits and positive attributes can be determined and tailor-made exercises applied to overcome any learning difficulties. This would require more resources that are presently allocated to children's welfare.

The aim of education is to develop all parts of the brain in appropriate ways for a child's stage of development, the Right Side all-rounder as well as the Left Side specialist, the Primal Brain practical as well as the Forebrain abstract. Education has played a critical role in social development and progress, but an imbalance in the masculine thinking that created the educational system will be reflected in the system itself and in a male-dominated society.

Left-Side Thinking:

Sue Palmer in *Toxic Childhood* comments that, "The politicians who now run education are all examples of high-functioning S-style systemising brains [ie Left Side] who did very well in the education system, and therefore value those gifts. But they seem unable to see how E-type [ie Right Side] nurture is necessary to release these gifts. Hence their conviction that putting very young children into cheap institutionalised childcare can somehow substitute for the experience of being brought up in a loving family".

Women, who tend to favour the Right Side, have been able over recent decades to rebalance the two Sides of the New Brain by also developing the Left Side skills of logic, analysis and detachment through a male-devised education system. They can now make better use of both Sides of their brains by integrating the different ways of thinking.

Women then can make best use of their Forebrains. It has been shown that women who receive education, particularly at higher level, go on to have smaller, healthier families and are encouraged to become entrepreneurs and leaders at local and national level.

A baby's brain recapitulates the story of mankind's history in its individual brain development, so it makes sense to model education on this pattern, going through the Ages in turn. First comes natural, instinctive learning; next learning the rules through developing the New Brain's Right Side, followed by more independent thought at senior school by applying principles to individual situations; and finally self-direction at degree level and above that develops the Forebrain's skills of responsibility and abstraction.

Then the cycle around the brain begins again with the newcomer learning to survive in a new work environment helped by the Primal Brain, becoming part of a bigger group, then striving to make your individual mark through the skills of the Left Side, even rising to the top - but then can come redundancy or retirement. And so the spiral around the parts of the brain continues and forms part of life-long education. Most education has a Left Side bias, but by contrast, the work of craftspeople tends to help them integrate the different parts of their brains.

Play:

Sue Palmer emphasises the importance to children's brain development of enriched play environments. Impoverished environments can restrict natural brain flexibility, just as rich or poor environments can affect social mobility. "Just like real food, real play - active, creative, social and outdoor - nourishes the natural development of body and brain." However, she notes that, "The home-grown, spontaneous, free play is no longer 'cool'. Children are so accustomed to a **battery reared** (my emphasis) existence, that they have handed over their imagination to the computer games manufacturers". It is adults as creators and purchasers of these games who are responsible for this situation.

Barbara Arrowsmith-Young's cognitive exercises in *The Woman Who Changed Her Brain* (many seemingly similar to traditional childhood games or activities) forge new neural pathways or mental constructs in the brain so that later concepts, such as maths, can be accommodated within the construct. For example, when a child is in a field and running to jump up and catch a branch, his brain unconsciously computes speed, distance, size, weight, height and probable risk-factor, amongst other things. This creates a 'maths' mental framework which helps makes sense of later information given in class. Watching someone do it on a screen does not have the same effect on the brain, however much parents want to protect their children from perceived stranger danger.

Dr Carol Dweck in her book *Mindset* advises parents not to protect children from the sadness of failure through constant praise but to, "Teach their children to love challenges, be intrigued by mistakes, enjoy effort and keep on learning. Praise what they accomplish through practice, study, persistence and good strategies". This encourages the greater use of the Forebrain, and a sense of self-worth based on reality by using mistakes as building blocks towards a long-term goal, and helps keep the ego from developing into an unrealistic Mighty I.

Accelerated Education:

Education encapsulates the millennia of mankind's learning into about 15 years or so, yet recently education has introduced computer use from today's world into very young children's worlds. What stages of brain development are being lost and which over-stimulated by this hot-housing or 'battery rearing'? Even the very early emphasis on Left Side symbolic skills of reading, writing and arithmetic means that some children are being 'force-fed' before they are ready naturally. Formal (or Left Side) education begins at 7 years old in many European schools, with every indication that they catch up and sometimes overtake children in the UK, who start formal education much earlier.

Many children's brains are linked at a very early stage today into an electronic network, so that some come to school unable to turn a page in a book, more used to swiping a screen. By contrast, an article in *The Times* on 5 October 2012 told how dogs in the classroom could help children with reading. This may be because the child and dog's Emotional Wheels link up to create an emotional not electronic network, and the child's stroking the dog releases tension and fear, calming the child and allowing the emotional energy to flow to and stimulate higher brain levels.

Under-development:

In the 60's there was a swing away from the very Left-Side rigidity of straight rows and over-emphasis on Primal Brain rote learning, but this has been replaced by teachers increasingly trying to fill the gaps left by the neglect of the socialising role of the family, where children need first to learn the rules of society and their place in it. Young people are showing us by their behaviour that something has gone wrong - very wrong in the case of the 2011 riots, which were chaotic, disordered, violent and destructive, fuelled by fiery eruptions of greed and organised by a network unavailable to the forces of law and order. This is a good description of the Underground Pit, as well as a lack of Forebrain supervision as we will see later. It is also an example of the mirroring between the brain and the social world.

How big a role does the Forebrain play in education? The Forebrain is the centre for imagination, creativity and spirituality; it is also the source of our culture, philosophy, arts and invention, all subjects often neglected in favour of Left Side skills of analysis and objectivity. Culture provides us with the opportunity to go beyond the world we experience in our own lives. What is required by all involved in education, including policy-makers, is a greater understanding of brain development, and then applying what is appropriate for each stage in to an integrated programme so that no child falls through the net and potentially through the trapdoor into the underworld of society.

Filling the Gap

I have referred above to teachers trying to fill the gaps left by underdeveloped or dysfunctional Right Side socialisation. How does the brain itself avoid having a gap if the two Sides of the New Brain have not developed to similar levels at the appropriate stages? Having a gap can make it easier for the Underground Pit's trapdoor to open and fill the space.

One way to fill the gap is for the Left Side to use its justifying skill we met in Section 1. By spreading itself out, it can ignore any gaps, just as one justifies a line in typing by spreading it out to keep the lines straight. The Left Side also uses this skill to justify an action when challenged by information it has ignored, usually from the Right Side that it has neglected, called as we saw earlier wilful blindness in law, or *anosognosia* in neuroscience.

Secondly, the gap can be reduced or eliminated by the more dominant Side 'colonising' the less developed side and assimilating or subverting its skills to fit into the dominant way of thinking. An example might be when some shops took over the 'green' initiative to reduce the number of plastic bags for environmental reasons, but subverted the original intention when they saw the opportunity to increase profits by reducing the number of bags they provided and by making customers pay for bags they used to receive for free. Another example might be that when a stronger Left Side, which tends to focus on objects, sees people as objects to be used, or when it assimilates the Right Side's bringing-together skill but uses it for 'things' rather than people, and so will collect paintings, antiques, even train numbers.

On the other hand, a stronger Right Side of the New Brain that has not developed Left Side skills to analyse things and take them to pieces, will assimilate the skill but apply it closer to home. So they may have lots of bits and pieces in the house or in their shop window, or perhaps instead of taking things to pieces, they take people and reputations apart in gossip or worse, causing divisions within families and communities.

Sometimes assimilating input or skills from the other side can become misappropriation if it is unacknowledged, like passing off information from the Internet as one's own work, or where contributions from other cultures are denied.

Thirdly, rather obviously, we can avoid having gaps by teaming up with someone with the opposite dominant Side in a relationship, when your partner can be literally your 'other half'. These brain differences do have a gender bias, with men favouring the Left Side of the New Brain and women favouring the Right Side, which have been re-inforced by society. Women used to stay at home within the family circle, while men went out to work in pinstripe suits or on production lines; today however, the roles can be reversed.

A partner can mirror our hidden parts, but what once caused a sense of wholeness or completeness can later cause conflict if one partner begins to develop their 'other' side for themselves. Divorce can sometimes be the only way for an individual to develop their own other half, and so integrate their inner two Sides more. If the aim of marriage was seen not as the joining of two halves but, as in education, of helping everyone develop internal integration, that would support family life. Sharing time between outside work and family care would then become the norm.

When partners are in the early 'in love' stage, their Emotional Wheels link up and become enmeshed rather like those of mothers and babies, but it can make later independent development difficult. "A woman's brain will begin stimulating the mirror neurons in her own circuit as if her husband's body sensations and emotions were hers. The female brain is a high-performance emotions machine, geared to tracking, moment-by-moment, the non-verbal signs of the innermost feelings of others", writes Louann Brizendine in *The Female Brain*.

If both partners are to develop their own inner integration, then some over-connected circuits might need to separate first, before being re-integrated in a new way or at a higher level, possibly with professional help.

REBALANCING

When the Two Sides of the New Brain do achieve a better balance, then people can make best use of their Forebrains. The Forebrain has long been seen as the site of humanity's most advanced and reasoned thinking. Many societies, like people, make greater use of their Forebrains as they mature. The Forebrain can foresee the consequences of our actions, and it is where emotional energy has reached the highest concepts we know in law and morality, those of justice, honour, responsibility and mercy.

Responsibility in law is based on the concept that when people do things, they intended the natural and probable consequences of their actions. On the other hand, those whose brains have not yet reached this stage of development, because of age, brain malfunction or circumstances, will need external supervision and support from those with more mature Forebrains, such as parents, teachers, mentors, probation officers or counsellors.

However, the path to reach the Forebrain's high spot is a long, slow and hard path, like training for the Olympics. The hotspot lights up when we get there, that sense of achievement of reaching your goal releases a natural 'high' - very different from the TV-style quick-fix in the shape of drink or drugs. Yet if the brain's natural path of development is blocked for any reason, for example if the earlier stages have been missed out or damaged, then this quick-fix shortcut may be the only way that many people can have peak experiences, particularly young people.

View from the Top

Now that we have taken the narrow, winding path to the brain's crown in the Forebrain, a journey that will be repeated many times during our lifetime, let's take a look at the differences between what the four parts of the brain see, how this can affect relationships, society and systems, by showing how one word can have a different meaning to each of the four parts.

I will use 'time' as an example, but there are many more I could have chosen. To the Primal Brain, time means "now, now, now", the infantile need for instant gratification. To the Right Side of the New Brain, it means cycles of seasons and anniversaries. To the Left Side, time means deadlines and efficiency, while to the Forebrain time can be lost in imagination, concentration and higher levels of awareness. When asked which part or parts we use most in the time-poor West today, many people say the Primal Brain's 'now, now, now' and Left Side's deadlines and efficiency. This is the rat run we have seen earlier. We need all the different ways of seeing time so that we are in the most appropriate 'gear' for any situation. Yet if this is how differently people can see time which can be measured, just think what the four parts of the brain - and the four corners of the globe - can do with a concept like God.

Work

We have looked at how the goal of education is to develop all parts of the brain, and this goal could be extended to the world of work. Instead of the huge disruption caused by organisations being privatised or taken into public ownership and then back again, could it be people who make the changes, by substituting an integrated pattern of work between private, public, personal and voluntary work, rather than a single career ladder?

This pattern would support flexible brain functioning, and if work inside and outside the home is shared between men and women, children are not the only ones to benefit. "We all gain if men share the childcare", was the headline of an article by Mary Ann Sieghart in the '*i*' newspaper on 14 May 2012. In business, it is claimed that American companies with the highest number of women on their management boards have a 53% higher return on equity, and a 66% higher return on invested capital than companies run by men. These figures are impressive, and tend to confirm the effect of educating women in Left Side skills.

This flexible pattern might also help rebalance the work force and pay inequalities too. One section of the work force being overworked and another being unemployed in society today is very strongly linked to an unbalanced way of thinking. If we are to change the way we work, so that everyone makes best use of their skills and abilities for individual development and for the benefit of society, it would mean some people letting go control and others taking greater initiative, and that will not be easy for either group.

Love or Money?

Even with integration and crossover of skills, we still need to recognise that different situations usually require a greater emphasis on a particular way of thinking and priorities. Businesses tend to focus on information-processing and profit, while the caring and service professions focus on people's progress. When you care for others, you give them some of your emotional energy to help them heal or grow. This is true of parents, mentors, therapists, teachers, nurses, carers and many others.

This exchange of energies means drawing on one's own inner reserves, and these can become depleted. When this happens, or when too many demands are made by overwork or too much information-processing (all those bureaucratic forms), then the autopilot takes over, decision-making is affected and people are unable to give the compassionate love that those who depend on them need.

It has been shown that love and money have different reward systems in the brain. If the financial reward system is dominant, then people suffer. "Experiments in Switzerland and Nevada reported that pay diminished respondents' sense of commitment to one another and to the community. We can be motivated by one driver at a time ... and market thinking has obliterated moral thinking on a grand scale", states Margaret Heffernan in *Wilful Blindness*. Another way of saying it is that you cannot serve the two masters of love and money equally. We need both, but one has to lead.

Balancing Old and New

When we have reached the goals that society has set, how do we feel? There can be a feeling of "Was that it?" that I saw once on a gravestone. The major opportunity for rebalancing, as we have seen, is during the midlife crossing. In the past, when men were drawn to that Crossing Bridge in midlife, they sometimes felt the need to step off the self-focused career ladder to spend more time with their grandchildren, gardening and supporting community activities, developing a sense of 'us' rather than 'I' alone in a cut-throat jungle. Derek Milne in his book *Coping With A Midlife Crisis* also highlights the positive side of the midlife crisis, "A distinctive priority for the future usually becomes the need to contribute to the lives of others and to accept one's social responsibilities".

It is as if one looks up, within, behind and ahead, making good use of the Forebrain's farseeing abilities to see the work still to do and want to give back to society. Some give their time to help others, others give money for good causes or give others the benefit of their experience, especially the young. There is often a strong bond between grandparents and grandchildren, as the Forebrain and Primal Brain re-connect. Could we not use this connection to involve older people more in teaching the young, giving purpose to the elderly and knowledge to the young?

Yet grandparents cannot do it all. Geraldine Bedell wrote in the *'i'* newspaper on 15 March 2013 that, "It's no exaggeration to say that the UK economy rests on the shoulders of grandparents. More than 60% of them - mostly grandmothers - are helping out with childcare, and if they weren't, parents wouldn't be able to work. British grandparents are twice as likely to be in paid work as their counterparts in other European countries. We are constantly being told that we are going to have to work longer to afford old age. This situation is unsustainable. Grandparents can't solve both the childcare problem and pensions problems. They are not superhuman." But they are undervalued.

The contribution made by older people is not always recognised, even when they retire. The figures show that far from being a burden on the state, retired people are net contributors. "Even when the bills for pensions, health and social care are taken into account, the balance sheet for the older part of the population is £40b in the black. By 2030, that net contribution is predicted to be almost double, as the baby-boomer generation reaches 65", according to *The Times* 2 September 2011. And with an ageing population, this could be good news.

INTEGRITY

Central to social integration is the concept of personal integrity and trust in each other. We saw in Chapter 4 how the role of the brain's Crossing Bridge is to integrate the different parts of the brain. With brain integration, we also have personal integrity, so that what we say is what we believe and also what we do. Here it is appropriate to use the translation of Wounded Body for *corpus callosum* because of its visual and symbolic associations. The image of a wounded body on the cross is Christian, part of the Western tradition, but the need for integration is universal. Without inner integration and personal integrity, we damage the Wounded Body at the brain's crossroads further. Religion calls this lack of integrity 'sin', while psychology calls this pain 'cognitive dissonance', or in more familiar language - hypocrisy. With integration, we have greater brain flexibility, just as greater social integration leads to less conflict, more social mobility and plurality.

So what is missing in our society today that makes personal integration difficult and creates a gap that some try to fill with things like money, power or possessions? What many feel is missing most in our world of individuality and the pursuit of personal gain is the final quarter of the Emotional Wheel - compassion. Most religions teach its importance and many people, such as Princess Diana, Mother Teresa and Nelson Mandela, have shown its role in their lives.

Compassion is not just for the poor or for victims, it is also needed for those who will find social change difficult, whether those having to let go their passive dependency or those used to being in a dominant position, who see other ways of thinking either as less important or as a threat to their identity. For some it will even seem like a form of death.

Elizabeth Kubler-Ross in her 1969 book *On Death And Dying* described the stages people go through when facing the prospect of death, and they are very similar to the 'spokes' of the Emotional Wheel we saw in Chapter 2. First there is the anger of rejection and denial at the news, believing that something will turn up to make everything alright again, but eventually resistance gives way, and down one goes into fear and hopelessness. It is here that many people get stuck and it is often only the compassion of others that helps them cross over into grief and the loss of all that might have been. Finally they reach their own compassion and acceptance.

What stage of change have we, as a society, now reached when many certainties seem to be dying: anger and denial, or fear and a sense of hopelessness - or are we ready to let go our dreams and accept that change may mean less materially rather than more? What is holding us back from facing the reality of the changes we need to make inside our heads and in the societies our brains create?

We can try to deny the need to change, just as some people deny the passing of time with botox and silicone but change is already happening. For example, the integrity of those in charge of society's major institutions is under examination as never before: the banking system, Parliament, BBC, hospitals and the media for example. There are changes in the social roles of men and women, with women moving into the market place and men caring for the children. The New IT, Integrated Thinking, offers a framework within which these and many other changes can be located, and which can make an uncertain future seem less threatening and more predictable.

CHAPTER REVIEW

In this chapter we have applied the framework developed in Section 1 on how the brain works to social development. We have looked at the roles the different parts of the brain play in various social activities and systems, in order to begin the process of seeing why society needs to change. We do not have to destroy social or political systems to make those changes: we can change the way we use them and our priorities, and so repeat the pattern of brain development of recycling old parts for new purposes.

In addition, reducing the role of automation by employing more people may reduce profit and competition, but it would also reduce the role of the auto pilot - and the welfare bill - while increasing social interaction and personal responsibility and therefore also increase the role of the Right Side of the New Brain and the Forebrain. It depends which is more important: money or people.

In the next chapter, we will extend the integration of personal and social development into the domain of politics in a market economy. Politics is about power, economics about money and the market is about possessions - all the things modern Western society seems to value.

6 POLITICAL DEVELOPMENT

We have seen how our present way of thinking is in reality many different ways, although one way can come to dominate, and that there can be conflict between the different ways. This is why we need to change our way of thinking to a more integrated model. In this chapter we are going to look at how the pattern of personal development can be replicated in the wider picture of political and economic development, for as they used to say in the Women's Movement: "the personal is political". Decision-making is critical to politics, and as we saw in Chapter 2, decisions are not just based on information; they also depend on emotional development. As in Chapter 5 on social development, the four main parts of the brain will guide the exploration in this chapter to see how personal and political development can be integrated into the New IT framework.

AUTO IN ACTION

We will be looking first at what are the roles that the Primal Brain plays in the world of politics and economics, in particular the Serpent's role in promoting the image of Man the Hunter, fuelled by the male hormone testosterone, the aggressive, active, aroused "tiger in the tank", which I call the T-effect. On average, the adult male body produces about 7-8 times more testosterone than the female body. Levels of testosterone are raised when men are aroused, compete, win, take risks or dominate, and when they see or take part in conflict, including political conflict, or are in pursuit of money, power, status or a mate.

The T-effect can be seen in economic brinkmanship, Britain's first-past-the-post electoral system, adversarial legal jousting, and even the baying in the bear-pit that the House of Commons sometimes resembles. Studies such as those by Nicholas Wright (see *Proceedings of Royal Society B* 2011) show that the T-effect makes people less co-operative and more egocentric; indeed some egotistical politicians have even gone so far as claiming that, 'L'Etat, c'est moi'.

It may have been behind the 'swinging d...' mentality of the phallocrats in the financial world with rising levels of testosterone feeding excessive, irrational risk-taking, but in today's financial crisis, that symbol of potency called 'growth' has taken a downward turn, and is looking distinctly flabby.

The biggest problem of the T-effect is that when the Primal Brain takes control, it shuts out the advanced skills of the Forebrain such as planning, foresight, self-control, responsibility and reasoned decision-making. This is not good for the political process or economic decision-making.

The Primal Brain is more dominant in children, who act out their emotions, so that if they are angry, they kick something; if they are frightened, they hide; when sad, they cry and when they feel sorry for something, they stroke it.

Then it appears that the brains of boys and girls take a different route. It seems that emotion and language become more integrated in girls' brains as they develop so that they can talk about their feelings and express them verbally, while boys stay focused on physical action to express emotion. Louann Brizendine explains that, "In the female brain, the circuit for aggression is more closely linked to cognitive, emotional and verbal functions than is the male aggression pathway, which is more connected to brain areas for physical action". Women use words to resolve differences rather than responding physically, but this over-articulation can overwhelm some men. Boys and men need help to overcome less developed brain pathways between words and emotional development in order to leave violence behind in relationships - and in the political peace process.

Emotions are not just an add-on app to human life. They have their foundation in the Primal Brain's Emotional Wheel but also reach our highest aspirations of human potential in the Forebrain. Particularly relevant to politics and economics is that without this higher level of emotional development, moral decision-making is difficult and so is empathy for the needs of others.

However, there has been a tendency to ignore, neglect or dismiss emotions, perhaps because in most men they do not occupy as much brain space as the T-effect of sexual arousal. Louann Brizendine again: "Volunteers viewed emotional images while having their brains scanned. Nine different areas lit up in women, but only two in men". Fewer women in public life compound this bias.

Nevertheless, there are signs of change. A recent study showed that men who spent more than three hours a day caring for children had the lowest T-effect scores. And we know that the feminine hormone oxytocin rises when caring for others, creating bonds, trust and compassion. Yet I cannot see men letting go the traditional adversarial style of politics and law or competition in the urban jungle without a fight - which will only increase the T-effect.

IN OPPOSITION

In early childhood, different areas of the brain act like land-grabbers carving out domains for their activities, with frequent raids into 'enemy' territory when the opportunity arises. This is particularly true of the Primal Brain, which has strong links throughout life with the land and the countryside.

Later the human brain creates more stable centres, with communication networks linking pathways between ideas or memories, and these pathways strengthen the more that they are used, while boundary conflicts lessen. In a similar way, early history was first dominated by territorial disputes; then as community settlements became stronger and were linked by pathways, societies grew and towns began to flourish.

Brain connections too cluster around key brain sites as children grow. These clusters grow bigger and better connected inside the brain as children develop, while in the world outside cities evolved and so did the need for greater organisation and structures, helped by (or perhaps led by) the development of the Left Side of the New Brain.

Democracy

It is the Left Side of the New Brain, typically more dominant in men, that draws lines and creates boundaries, and so it was men who created political systems that drew the lines about how to run life in the city or 'polis', while laws defined the boundaries about what was acceptable behaviour and what was not, who was responsible and the appropriate outcome. In a sense, laws codified the Forebrain's control over the Primal Brain, and the resolution of disputes between opposing sides.

In the beginning, it was a few powerful individual men who had strengthened their position by acquiring power and territories who made the political decisions, but in Ancient Greece, the people rose up and showed that they too wanted to play a part in the decision-making, and so democracy developed. Different countries reach this stage at different times, and in some countries even today, it is still only a few men who have crossed the bridge to independence and personal decision-making and are reluctant to give up their dominance. They block the way for others to follow like kings in the animal jungle will see off threats to their supremacy. Another situation where animal-like aggression can be roused is the killing in families of the offspring of other males.

Yet it is sometimes forgotten how recently it was in the UK that slavery was abolished, that women had the vote and could take out a loan without a male signatory and children were protected and no longer worked in factories. In a Left-Side dominated world, it takes time for concern for others to catch up with increasing power, and for human rights to catch up with the freedom of a market economy.

Party Lines

Today, democracy in Britain is made up of four main parts, like the brain (see Figure 1): there is the 'country' or voters who elect the Members of Parliament, the two sides of the House of Commons like the two Sides of the New Brain, and the House of Lords. There is the speaker trying to keep order between the two opposing sides, which often seem to find it difficult to see the other's point of view, each justifying its own actions, resorting to an immature tribal allegiance along party lines so often seen in party politics.

On the one side are the Conservatives with a focus on the world of business, initiative and standing on one's own two feet, while on the other side is socialism or Labour supported by groups of workers, focusing on public services and the protection of weaker members of society. You may recall that it is the Left Side of the New Brain that controls the right side of the body, so those in politics who favour Left Side attributes such as private enterprise, the independence of the individual and personal ownership are on the political 'Right'; while those who work for the needs of the group, such as trade unions and public ownership, are on the political 'Left'. And so there are the great opposites in politics of Conservatism or Socialism, Capitalism or Communism.

There are swings in a democracy between one side and the other, which might create balance over time but not harmony because of the conflict between the two sides, and as with our brains, small differences can have a big outcome if in key sites in deciding who wins the struggle for supremacy. The UK election of 2010 showed that people wanted greater integration in the political process.

So into the picture came the Liberal Democrats, marginalised no longer, but having their untried idealism put to the test. The link between Forebrain and Primal Brain, ideas and reality, seems to be weak when creating policies sometimes, so that new policy initiatives are promoted without first consulting those on the ground with practical knowledge, leading to political U-turns.

Christopher Lasch points out in *The Minimal Self* that concepts from psychoanalysis (eg the superego, ego, and id, and the importance of mouth, bowel and phallus bodily functions in early personality development) provide an insight into the political landscape. "The Conservatives regard the restoration of the superego, strong parental authority, as the best hope for social stability. For others, it is the ego, the rational faculty, that needs to be strengthened, which is the essence of the liberal, humanist tradition ... while the new left's politics begin with feelings". Other analysts see war and military technology, space rockets and ballistic missile rivalry as all too clearly embodying a contest of insecure penises out to prove their size and potency. The same could be said of the financial markets.

Boundary Changes
Working together in coalition is just one of a series of recent national and international changes in politics, all leading towards greater integration both in the brain and in the systems the brain has created in the outside world.

In education, there used to be a division between boys studying science and girls studying literature, while there was a division of labour between men and women. There was men's work and there was women's work, but the Women's Movement changed the boundary lines. Women moved into anger and into men's worlds, to make long-lasting personal, social, political and legal changes, leaving the hippies to their communal "all you need is love", back-to-nature idealism.

So, in the 70's, women moved from their traditional group stronghold of the family into territories previously held by men, as they moved from the Right Side of the New Brain into the Left Side. Hungry for power, they learnt how to deal with big business and about financial markets. Some men were angry or in denial, others became more extreme, but a brave few crossed back over the bridge into caring for the family, from individuality to the group.

The greater individual freedoms of the liberal revolution were followed by the financial freedoms of the market revolution in the 80's, as described by David Lammy in *Out Of The Ashes*, and the personal did indeed become political as women had proclaimed. In the 90's, New Labour followed the women's lead and moved from **its** traditional group stronghold of the unions into territories held by the Conservatives. Hungry for power, they too learnt how to deal with big business and financial markets. Tory reactions to New Labour were similar to the earlier ones of men to the Women's Movement - anger, denial, rejection - but a brave few were willing to cross over the bridge from individuality into 'compassionate conservatism'.

In neither the social nor political revolutions was the move in the opposite direction equally balanced, either by men moving into the home or by Tories moving into compassionate conservatism, and it is this imbalance which is examined in detail by Hannah Rosin in *The End of Men*.

Initially, the move by women into the world of work and politics was seen as a challenge to men and to their world, but as the women tried to fit themselves into systems devised by men, they became assimilated into the market place, just as the dominant Side of the New Brain will assimilate skills from the other side and so increase its dominance. Minor changes were made to accommodate women's additional role in the family, but major changes were being made in women's brains, as we will see later.

New Labour went overboard in welcoming those with money and power, increasing Left Side dominance even further, like the collapse of communism left capitalism as almost the only game in town. And globally too, the traditional importance of the group in the East is being eroded by western individualistic ways of thinking and behaving. Finally capitalism, a system for making and selling 'things', is itself under extreme pressure, and so are the people who try to fit their own personal development into a framework devised for things.

Imbalances

These men/women, Conservative/Labour, West/East changes are leading to an overweight Left Side, often literally, which takes most of the resources from the other parts of the brain. Similarly, the world is being depleted of resources to feed the growing demands of capitalism, while there is an obesity epidemic in the West at the same time that people are starving in developing countries. In addition, the demand for individuality and personal choice is leaving vulnerable even those in the UK who depend on the group - the young, the old, the sick - while reducing investment in public services and social housing.

In Chapter 5, we saw how this imbalance is reflected in those who are employed being overworked, while the number of people unemployed is increasing, especially in some European countries. Sir Richard Branson in an interview in *The Times* on 17 December 2011 said, "It is wrong that some people are in full time work, and others are out of work. Let's share the work around". His suggestions included more job-sharing (especially for those with young children) and moving to a 4-day working week. Immigrants coming from less developed societies to fill economic gaps can be a reflection of gaps in personal and socio-political development.

Those with a family background of dependency have problems leaving group security. The problem is reversed for many whose dependency on the family group was cut short by being sent to boarding schools, and then often going to Oxbridge, and who are over-represented in positions of power. They had to learn to stand on their own two feet outside the family circle, usually in an all-male environment, years before the normal time for this stage of development, sometimes envious of siblings or other children still at home. In order to survive, they had to reject the dependency side of themselves, and so have a tendency to reject or criticise those who are still dependent. Sometimes that earlier envy is re-activated into attacks on 'stay-at-home scroungers'.

Because the basic need for dependency in the public school/Oxbridge groups may not have been fully met or had to be denied in order for them to survive, becoming part of a group-based system later can be seen as a threat to their mental construct and become a bit of a bogey man: reds in their beds, a health care system that smacks of socialism in USA or joining the European Union. Even getting married and having a family can be a threat to their 'independence'.

This is not a condemnation of men or the systems and structures that their way of thinking has devised, for without them, we would not have reached our present stage of development. However the dominance of the Left Side's way of thinking may no longer be as appropriate as it once was, and dominance of any one part makes Integrated Thinking more difficult. Some are ready to move on to the next stage.

Moving On

Women have now developed Left Side skills through education, business and personal choice, and this helps them analyse critically the models on which politics, society and work are based, beginning with the deconstruction of patriarchy in the 70's. Now that most women work outside the home as well as in it, they have time to experience life on the other side and many are moving back to take a more balanced position between personal achievement and caring for others, the so-called better work/life balance - and so are many younger men.

These changes affect the way women think too. Mona Lisa Schultz in *The New Feminine Brain* points out that, "The feminine brain today is not your grandmother's brain. For the last 50 years, women have had to accommodate [or integrate] two divergent roles, and our brains had to re-wire themselves to adapt. When women learn to juggle traditional feminine roles with newer, once typical male responsibilities, their brains change, giving unique gifts and abilities". This inner rebalancing can only help create a better balance in society and a different kind of politics.

The more integrated the different parts of our brains are, the more integrity we have in whatever we do, including politics. Joan Smith's article in the *'i'* newspaper on 6 September 2012 echoed this need for politics to benefit from these new brains, saying, "I don't want speeches from politicians' wives. All I want is more women becoming politicians in their own right". While Barbara Tuchman in *The March of Follies* believes that, "The problem may not be so much about a matter of educating officials for government, as educating the electorate to recognise and reward integrity of character".

We have looked at the connections between society and politics and the brains of those who created their systems and structures, and at how this is changing. But despite all the changes, the market remains a law unto itself, and the same theory of human nature based on the autopilot/hunter/Serpent model still underpins the free market: man as self-interested robot, maximising events to his advantage. Yet when this model was tested recently, it was found to be seriously flawed, as it seemed to apply only to economists, psychopaths and Cold War game-players. It is a model that needs changing.

AUTHORITY

We have been looking at how the human brain appears to use its own internal workings as a template for the social and political systems and structures that it has created. Politics is concerned with making decisions and laws, and it is the development of the mature Forebrain that is critical in creating the highest concepts we know in law and morality.

Frans de Waal in *Our Inner Ape* reminds us that moral and legal decision-making is driven by emotions. By this he means not the raw emotions of early development, but those that have reached the top of the Tree of Life in the mature Forebrain (see Figure 3). In the English legal system, we see the development of the Forebrain both in the role of judges and the House of Lords.

In his book *Letters to Lily*, Alan Macfarlane explains the particular role that English law has played in the development of concepts of individuality and trust in our society. "The assumption of individual rights is a very old feature of English Law. Very few societies shared this view. Almost everywhere else, the family is the foundation upon which society is built."

He also points out the importance of trusts, developed in mediaeval times as a way of avoiding land being forfeited back to the crown, but which have had an impact beyond their original intention. "The whole system of devolved government, the shires with their magistrates, the parish councils etc were given strength by the concept of 'trusts'. Local educational and church organisations were trust-based. In democracy, power is held in trust for the people." The independence of the judges marked a critical stage in English Law. Lord Denning states in *Landmarks Of The Law*, "It is cardinal in our Constitution that judges are independent of the government. They do not give advice to the government on points of law or fact: nor do they receive it."

Legal trials have similarities with our own internal decision-making, but on a much longer time-scale. Just as we make decisions by reference to a moral code (the advanced levels of the Tree of Life) and after considering information from both Sides of the New Brain, so a judicial decision is made based on a code built up over time, when information from both sides of the case has been considered. The outcome of both internal and judicial decision-making is to increase responsibility for our actions and so enhance the use of our Forebrains.

In the past, the Forebrain was the authority of the elders, usually men, passing on the tribe's knowledge and decision-making from generation to generation, and who created the systems associated with patriarchy that had to be obeyed, rather in the way that tradition has dominated in the past. This is very different from the self-directed mature development of today's Forebrain.

The Forebrain is sometimes described as the brain's 'executive', but often this role is played in adulthood by the New Brain, just as in politics it is undertaken by the government in power, while the House of Lords, unlike in previous centuries, now merely amends, postpones or asks the lower House to reconsider.

The House of Lords is made up of hereditary peers (those aristocratic early territorial winners) and bishops, with newer members appointed for their distinguished careers. The bishops could be said to represent the Forebrain's 'Godspot' referred to in Chapter 1, but also to reflect the role that Christianity has played in the law-making process. Lord Denning again: "A great change was made by the Judicature Acts 1873. The rules of law and equity were fused together. Whenever there was any conflict between them, the rules of equity were to prevail". The Law of Equity is derived in part from old Church law, so the Act gave precedence to what is right and proper from the Law of Equity over the importance of rights and property under the common law.

In Britain, the Monarch is the head of State, Church and Parliament, in whose name all laws are made. Rather than the pursuit of power, the Monarch symbolises a life of service and duty to the common good, which is very much in keeping with the Forebrain's role. We call the top of the head the 'crown' too. "The British Monarchy", Andrew Marr remarks in *Diamond Queen*, "is a slight oddity among her natural allies and partners - the republics of the United States, France, Germany, India and Pakistan, never mind China, Brazil and Russia". Although the monarchy represents continuity, he notes that, "Monarchy is a perpetual act of reinvention".

There have been some changes to the House of Lords too in recent years, exchanging some of the aristocracy for people from a wider background, those who have worked outside the Westminster 'bubble' and who know how things work - or do not work - in the real world, as well as experienced former MPs.

The restructuring of the House of Lords could be likened to the rewiring of the Forebrain in maturity, although some would like the process to be more radical, and questions remain about the role of the Anglican Church in Parliament and the State.

In the model I am using to integrate political development with the framework of personal development, there seems to be a case for the House of Lords having more power rather than less and for greater diversity by having more women and more representatives from ethnic groups on its seats. Similarly, a greater role for modern-day elders, so different from their ancient forebears who relied on custom and obedience for their position, could be reflected in other decision-making bodies, such as the European Union and the United Nations.

BETTER DECISION-MAKING

It is clear that the best decision-makers are those who have integrated all parts of themselves, balancing information-processing with emotional development, and who have integrity. Yet it is also clear that overwork or stress can lead to more automatic, less compassionate decisions and this can apply to leaders especially those who become isolated from reality, surrounded by a small clique. Some revert to earlier, less modulated beliefs despite election promises.

As we saw earlier, it is the Crossing Bridge or Wounded Body in the brain that integrates all the different parts so that we have personal integrity. Without integrity, there is internal 'cognitive dissonance' - rather like uproar in the House of Commons. The dissonance or conflict between a politician's public role and his private life can result in a fall from power, often because Primal Brain drives have taken control, with a lack of regulation from the Forebrain.

And because of the gap between their information processing and moral development, this lack of integration and regulation brings their decision-making into question. Political journalists attack any split between politicians, or between public and private images, just as the unconscious can attack any gap in our development, delighting in pointing out mistakes. It now seems the media have influenced decision-making more than we realised, and compromised the law makers and enforcers, just as elements within the unconscious can influence and compromise us.

How can one tell what stage of socio-political development a nation has reached? Mikhail Gorbachev said that one could tell by the position of its women: are they fully integrated into social and political life, or are they marginalised, even excluded? Margaret Thatcher epitomised those earlier women who moved into the world of men and adopted their model of working; she was sometimes referred to as the 'best man in the cabinet'. Now women are finding a new way of leading, not tied to the male model.

To the question of whether the world would be more peaceful if women were in charge, Steven Pinker gives a qualified 'yes' in *The Better Angels Of Our Nature*. He states that, "Men are, of course, by far the more violent sex," and that, "A recognition of women's rights and an opposition to war go together. Several surveys have found that the better a society treats its women, the less it embraces war".

It is not only older people who have had the chance to integrate different parts of themselves. It is like with most things, the sooner you start and the more you do it, the easier it gets. So political leaders who have lived in different countries, learned other languages or experienced different ways of doing things, are more adaptable to change. They have made best use of the brain's built-in flexibility, and can encourage others to believe they can change too, but perhaps without realising how difficult change can be for those who have not had the benefit of their experiences.

Scientists have discovered that the brain remains flexible well into old age and the more new things you experience, the more flexible it remains. It seems there is no truth in the old saying that you can't teach an old dog new tricks. In fact, he might be able to teach you a thing or two!

CHAPTER REVIEW

In this chapter we have seen how the four main parts of the brain and inner integration 'play out' in politics, bringing the personal and the political into the same developmental framework. Change can start within so that the brain creates a different world on the outside, or vice versa. This is similar to how the law works: it can respond to changes in society or create them, as it has done in the fields of anti-discrimination or human rights law.

So what does need to change in the political world? Capitalism, the sole survivor of the battle of ideas with communism, is the best system we have had so far for money and things, but a system for objects is not necessarily a good system for people. Only an extreme Left Side of the New Brain would think that.

An alternative would be to use the more appropriate human life cycle as the basis for personal, social and political growth, instead of the economic cycle. "Growth is the eternal mandate of the Mind", claimed Robert Ornstein. It seems that this kind of growth has been assimilated or subverted by Left Side thinking to mean material and economic growth in the world outside.

The brain is very good at re-using old parts for new purposes, and we will need to copy this as we develop Integrated Thinking. This addresses the question sometimes raised of what happens to old ways of thinking when we change to a new way - they are not lost or discarded but given a new lease of life in a different role. The same could apply to economics so that it plays a supporting role in human development, rather than dominating it.

Capitalism is just one of many systems that people have made up, and like all the systems people have created, the unconscious plays a role. It too has to find an appropriate place in a new way of thinking about politics and law.

7 THE UNDERWORLD

We saw in Chapter 6 how the brain draws on the development of greater Forebrain jurisdiction over the Primal Brain in the creation of the legal system and law enforcement. We have also seen in Chapter 3 how the Underground Pit operates within its own twisted rules, just as the criminal underworld twists the rule of law.

The police force is the 'thin blue line' that patrols the boundary separating the criminal underworld from the world above. When alerted, police rush to the scene of conflict or collision to contain it, or act swiftly when underworld elements break the legal code, to ensure the security of the whole system. In brain development, I referred to this adrenalin-fuelled area as the safety net, and the entrance to the Underground Pit of the unconscious as the trapdoor, usually operating below our conscious awareness.

CRIME

There are many similarities between the underworld and the world of the unconscious Underground Pit. Criminal activity can be opportunistic, but it has tended to become more and more organised; this reflects the pattern of brain development I have called the 'rat run' between the Gut Brain, the Serpent of the Primal Brain and the Left Side of the New Brain. The Mighty I is seen in many Big Men at the head of criminal gangs, such as the Mafia Godfathers. This world is so twisted that some criminals call revenge 'honour', and misappropriate Forebrain skills such as planning, so that evolution is turned on its head, with the most primitive parts of the brain dominating the more developed.

The criminal underworld is fuelled by those twisted emotions of venomous hatred, terrorism, revenge and obsessions of the Underground Pit, and the greed for money, power and possessions. It can leak out in crime, violence and rage everywhere like contaminating nuclear waste, but the real waste is in lost people and lost lives.

English Law presumes that people intend the natural and probable consequences of their actions, but as we have seen, this foresight does not fully develop until after late adolescence. So where does legal responsibility for one's actions stand if the Forebrain does not develop even in adulthood, or is damaged because of earlier experiences or malfunction? In his book *Change Your Brain, Change Your Life*, Daniel Amen proposes that, "If a [defendant] does not have the capacity for internal supervision that is housed in the [Forebrain], legal authorities may have to compose external supervision in some form of contained setting". That is, until such time as he develops internal supervision or self-control for himself. The question has to be asked why the Forebrain of those who break the law did not take over at the appropriate time from their Primal Brain, unconscious and Gut Brain, which continued to dominate instead of being relegated to playing a supporting role?

Steven Pinker in *The Better Angels Of Our Nature* believes that, "The main reason that violence correlates with low socio-economic status today is that the elites and middle classes pursue justice within the legal system while the lower classes resort to what scholars of violence call 'self-help'. It is another name for vigilantism, frontier justice, taking the law into your own hands and other forms of violent retaliation by which people secured justice in the absence of intervention by the state". Self-help justice may have been all that was available once, but is no longer appropriate in today's West. To change it requires a handover of power from the individual to the state (and access to justice at all levels of society), and the handover of power from the unconscious level of revenge to the Forebrain of justice and mercy.

If higher levels of brain control have not been developed or emotions linked to language, then people can tend to 'act out' their emotions. We can then use this knowledge to address inappropriate behaviour both for individuals and for society as a whole. One of the human system's biggest disadvantages is that the critical first years are governed by the unconscious. It is only through a child's actions and later adult behaviour that experts can begin to understand what happened to interrupt or corrupt the evolutionary pattern of brain development, and then use the brain's flexibility to develop new patterns.

Prison could provide opportunities to re-start and correct this uncompleted programme and encourage a greater use of the Forebrain's sense of responsibility, foresight and moral maturity. Locking people up without using the time to help them progress is like trying to contain unwanted elements of our own personality or emotions in the Underground Pit: in the long run, it does not work and can make things worse.

For at the base of the Underground Pit and the underworld is the subhuman and inhuman world of corruption, sadism and destruction that infiltrates the world above through cracks in the surface, just as fiery outbursts of volcanoes from earlier stages of the earth's development can explode into the atmosphere and darken the skies.

Some police patrolling the boundary line can slip below the net into the Underground Pit. Certain aspects of political decision-making have also been affected, with politicians becoming too closely associated with the media, big business or lobbyists. Tom Watson in the phone-hacking debate in the House of Commons on 10 September 2010 claimed that, "They, the barons of the media, with their red-top assassins, are the biggest beasts in the jungle. They have no predators. They are untouchable. They laugh at the law. They have the power to hurt us, and they do with joy and criminality." An indication that 'taking the law into their own hands' is not restricted to lower socio-economic classes.

TV AND ONLINE

Closer to home, we all enter the unconscious world at night in our dreams or nightmares, but increasingly we see more of this world on television as well as in books and on film. Television, the far-seeing eye, was set up to inform, entertain and educate. Although acting like a mind's eye on the outside world, many TV programmes also open the trapdoor into the world below, and not only in its focus on detective and murder stories. Even within its own organisation, there is evidence of the abuse of power over staff and young people who had contact with the Mighty I's of fame and fortune.

The unconscious stores the stock characters that guide us and help us understand how people work. For many children, the dysfunctional families and communities of TV soaps are the social norms they are viewing and copying. What they see is what they do; it is how they learn about the world around them.

Nick Read writes in *Sick and Tired*, "Although the plots of soap operas cover a wide variety of social issues, the main characters are scripted to react to life situations in the most dysfunctional ways. Thus TV mirrors the distorted perceptions of a narcissistic society, in which image takes priority over community and personal values. We obtain a vicarious thrill from the dilemmas of the characters we see on the screen and are encouraged to mimic their confrontational attitudes".

TV soaps possibly also reflect an increasingly autistic society. Dr Becky Heaver in an article on Asperger's Syndrome in *The Times* 12 May 2012 said that, "I sometimes wonder if my interest in TV soaps is related to my Asperger's. Soaps are about social relationships but they are exaggerated. When an actor is feeling emotion, he or she acts very clearly and there is music. That makes it very clear to me what's going on". It is possible that the television screen compensates for the mirror cells that help us feel what others are feeling which seem to under-perform in those on the autistic spectrum.

The BBC is a public body, paid for by a licence fee. It is said we get the politicians we deserve, and that may be also true of television programmes, but children do not deserve to have their development twisted by what we pay for them to watch.

Recent studies have shown that early exposure to television between the ages of one and three years old is associated with problems in paying attention and controlling impulses in later childhood. However other studies would indicate that there are additional factors involved; for example, children of more socially-deprived families tend to watch more television and spend more time playing computer games. Perhaps relying on an outside screen means children do not develop their own inner screen, the mind's eye in the Forebrain, that helps focus attention and control lower level impulses?

Sue Palmer in *Toxic Childhood* points to an even more disturbing effect, when images do stimulate viewers' mirror cell responses. "Neuroscientists have found that horrific pictures affect the emotional centres in the brain. The majority of TV news and many programmes are negative, depicting issues such as conflict and abuse. Over 1000 studies overwhelmingly point to a causal connection between media violence and aggressive behaviour in children. Psychologists believe that for children under 10 years of age, much of the stuff they now view and hear is frightening, worrying and emotionally destabilising, rather like living in a war zone".

The Primal Brain habituates to the stimuli it receives; it desensitises children to violence that they then copy, but also arouses anger and fear that have to be released. This response is seen in adults too. A detailed study into soldiers returning from Iraq and Afghanistan confirm they are more likely to commit violent crimes at home if they have witnessed traumatic events during active combat (*'i'* newspaper 15 March 2013). Releasing tension onto others is one way the unconscious deals with too much overload.

Sue Palmer says quite simply that the world we have created is damaging our children's brains. I do not believe that any civilised society sets out to damage its children consciously, but we have to think seriously about what kind of world we do want to see portrayed on screen: the civilised world of more evolved thinking and behaving, or the unconscious world of fantasy, nightmare and murder. Unfortunately, television is not the only way in which the unconscious can come to dominate life today. It has also entered the world of finance.

THE BOTTOM LINE

The Primal Brain at the base of the skull relies on ancient, inherited systems from previous ages to keep us alive. It gets its information from all over the body and works hard to balance supply and demand. However, as we have seen, there is another even more primitive brain at work in our guts. It can operate independently of the head brain, below our awareness and with a mind of its own. Before we can change anything, the Gut Brain has to be put in its proper place, and that is below, not above, the higher levels of human brain development.

We have seen how the Gut Brain was in control before birth, and it remains an instant feedback response that bypasses the usual thinking processes throughout life in our gut reaction. To recap on its early role: the developing foetus was fed and its waste taken away by his mother's blood through the umbilical cord connecting the baby's gut to the mother's placenta.

At birth, when a baby takes his first breath, the Gut Brain has to start the handover of control to the head brain. Pierre Pallardy describes the Gut Brain in *Gut Instinct*. "The abdomen is both structurally and neuro-chemically a 'second brain'. The neurons of the second brain have a life of their own. We have to sever the link between the two brains at about two years of age and move from the unconscious self to the social self."

It seems as if sometimes this handover does not go smoothly, even from the beginning. Michel Odent, the French doctor who coined the term 'Primal Brain', believes that if the break between the womb and the outside world is too sudden, the baby's head brain cannot adjust to the overwhelming sensory input of bright lights, noise, harsh treatment, and so it retreats. Gentle birthing was his recommendation. We still can react the same way when woken suddenly with noise and bright lights, and want to retreat back under the warm, dark covers. Imagine that magnified a million times for a newborn baby, and we can see how the Gut Brain could possibly be the fall-back situation and continue its pre-birth dominant role.

The Gut Brain's way of working dates from a time before there was oxygen on earth, just stinking swamps. It still avoids contact with oxygen now by residing in our guts. After birth, the Gut Brain's main role is to perform the essential dirty work in our intestines of breaking down material, separating things out, taking what it needs to recycle and discarding the rest - rather as we are encouraged to do with household waste today.

The Gut Brain also keeps part of the energy to feed itself, like retaining profits to feed the capitalist system. This link between the Gut Brain and money has a long history, even before William Gladstone said in 1858, "Finance is the stomach of the country". In the unconscious world, money is linked to the Gut Brain, and in a consumer society, the Gut Brain is king.

If the gut takes too much energy for itself, it can unbalance the whole system, in the same way that bankers' bonuses or tax avoidance schemes can unbalance the economy. The Gut Brain is the lowest on the brain chain but when connected to unregulated Primal Brain appetites, it can fuel an unsustainable lifestyle, obesity and greed. As Jonathan Porritt says of the West today in *Capitalism*, "We need things consumed, burned up, worn out, replaced and discarded at an every-increasing rate".

An obsession with consumption is part of the neural superhighway I call the 'rat run'. It is the Left Side of the New Brain that has created the capitalist system, and given the market human characteristics - the so-called guiding hand - while seeing people as 'things' or objects. When the rat run reached a critical supercharged mass, it seems to have created a world dominated by "I, NOW, MORE", and a narcissistic, short term, 'greed is good' way of thinking.

When the Gut Brain's programme for processing consumed goods permeates the Left Side of the New Brain, it can then be applied to people, who are seen as waste or as 'collateral damage'. This primitive programme is also activated when a market predator makes a hostile takeover, as he separates out the different parts of the company, takes what he wants and discards the rest of the workforce on the waste heap in the name of financial efficiency. Torturers also extract information from people in ways that are similar to the Gut Brain's programme for extracting nutrition from food: break them down, take what you want then dump them.

Christopher Lasch uses the psychoanalytical model in *Minimal Self* to show the link between society and early stages of development. "If 19th century bourgeois culture re-inforced anal patterns of behaviour - hoarding of money and supplies, control of bodily functions, control of emotion - the 20th century culture of mass consumption recreates oral patterns rooted at an even earlier stage of development, when the infant was completely dependent on the breast". Steve Jones in *The Serpent's Promise* says, "Junk food is a synthetic version of mother's milk. That may be why it is so addictive". It also activates baby-like dependency responses.

The Gut Brain plays a very big role in a consumer society and a bipolar-like boom or bust, feast or famine economy. It links in to the Primal Brain's role of monitoring the body's fluctuating blood sugar levels and energy supply, anticipating demand, replicated as the stock exchange outside, and recently the financial world has been involved in investing in some very dodgy sub-primal schemes.

It is essential to any new way of thinking that we have our different brains in the right order, and make sure the tail is not wagging the dog. The Gut Brain and its way of doing things have to come last. One way is to make it work harder at what it is supposed to do by giving it more unprocessed food to deal with, which has the added benefit of giving more nourishment to higher brain levels. More oxygen through outdoor activity also plays a part in keeping it under control and boosting higher brain levels. Similarly, the Primal Brain needs to do more of what it does best too, rather than outsourcing its automatic processing work to machines like calculators and computers, especially in childhood.

MONEY

Bacteria in the foul-smelling bogs ruled the earth before oxygen. They still do rule, in our guts. We have seen how the primitive Gut Brain operates like an independent processing centre. All along the bowels' serpentine length, bacteria take what is whole, break it down, use what they want, and discard the rest. This is a very necessary programme when applied to food, but deadly as we have seen when applied to people in pogroms, genocide or holocausts, sometimes even in the name of greater economic growth.

The Gut Brain's processes can infiltrate our thinking, just as digestive processes can flow back up, or even leak into our bloodstreams. The unconscious links waste products with money, bowel control with financial control, and this link is reflected in the words we use: doing the business, the bottom line; 'where there's muck there's brass' and so on. Psychologists say that people stuck at a developmental stage of over-rigid toilet training have 'anal personalities', and their characteristics are the four P's: Petty-Minded, Pompous, Penny-pinching and Prudish - and perhaps even prudent. Tight-fisted in other words. Is there some basic biology at work here that links bowel retention with greater pleasurable stimulation of the prostate gland, that male redundant equivalent of the female womb?

Yet, despite what some think, money is not the purpose of work, it is only a by-product, just as the by-product of eating is not its purpose. The purpose of food, work, relationships and life itself is to help us grow and progress as people. If we live to eat, instead of eat to live, we know we are in the twisted, back-to-front world of the Gut Brain. It is the same if money is our goal in life. We have seen how love and money have different reward systems in the brain. We need both but in the right order if we are to build a new way of thinking: things, including money, have to support people and information-processing has to support our progress as human beings, not the other way round.

When money is god, the Gut Brain is in control. A baby's cry for "more, more, more" is elevated into global greed. A toddler's potty battle when he refuses to perform can be repeated later in sit-in strikes or passive aggression; or his holding onto what he produces or else create a mess becomes the terrorists' threats to stockpile and use their stinking bombs of destruction. When these primitive processes are in control, they work without the moderating influence of mature brain development. We need mature thinking and decision-making to lead us, not the consuming mentality of money-making, greed and power.

CHAPTER REVIEW

In this chapter we have seen that there are similarities between the criminal and financial worlds with the Unconscious Pit, and that reversing the importance of different parts of the brain is fundamental to changing our present way of thinking so that less evolved parts no longer dominate. It will be difficult for us all, and may be particularly hard for those who thought that money-makers were the masters of the universe.

Before we leave this Section, however, we will look briefly at what anti-social behaviour tells us about individual and social development, and how it too can be integrated into the New IT.

8 ANTI-SOCIAL BEHAVIOUR

We are all born 'anti-social' as babies, although most learn the rules of society as children and live within them as adults. Some choose to break those rules, or perhaps never learnt them, and the result can be anti-social behaviour. Although anti-social behaviour tends to be associated with young people and/or criminal activity, some adults behave in ways that are damaging to society yet they are highly regarded and well paid.

However, as with everything in human development, there can be positive as well as negative aspects to anti-social behaviour, for example the impact of those risk-taking 'black sheep' who found their way to the colonies, including the United States of America, or those who challenged Authority over the slave trade or in favour of votes for women. A society where everyone obeys the rules is a society of automatons that does not change.

MIGHTY I

In the last chapter, we saw how the Gut Brain can link up with the Serpent of the Primal Brain and the Left Side of the New Brain to create a the rat run between them, so that the 'I' or ego becomes a predator in the market, driven by greed and by the pursuit of money, power and possessions. When this happens, the socialising Right Side of the New Brain and society's rules are neglected or even rejected. Psychopaths are at the extreme end of this spectrum of anti-social behaviour, but not all psychopaths are criminals; some are in highly successful positions of power.

Childhood is the appropriate stage to begin the socialising process - indeed it could be seen as one the primary aims of family life. Before two years of age, the Primal Brain of habit, repetition and copying is very strong, so this is when good habits can be encouraged, including copying what older siblings or parents do.

After about two years old, a toddler begins to map out in his mental constructs his own place in the wider scheme and to work out where he fits in. If he is treated like a little emperor, with every wish fulfilled, then that is what he thinks he is. Psychologists call this infantile omnipotence. If he is not given developmentally appropriate guidelines on what is expected of him, but instead allowed to choose everything - what to eat, do and wear and so on - then the "me, me, me, now, now, now" infantile stage can link directly to the immature 'I' of individual choice.

If this continues, then adapting to others and reality becomes more and more difficult as the ego is no longer the 'I' of individuality, identity and independence, dealing with reality, but has become a overgrown Mighty I, taking over more and more territory within the brain, and often in the outside world too. Growth, size and being bigger than the next man - we all can guess what drives that obsession. Steve Taylor in *Waking From Sleep* comments that, "The overdeveloped ego is the root cause of many of our social pathologies, including warfare, male domination, social inequality and oppression".

A Mighty I is like an overblown bubble with a leak, always needing to be pumped up by having followers do its bidding and so maintain its delusion of infantile omnipotence. These followers are usually people whose immature egos have not detached from earlier group dependency, so they need to attach themselves to someone stronger, or to a new group or an ideology. This is a natural stage of development at adolescence, when critical faculties are still developing, but it is also why young people are particularly susceptible to cult leaders and corporate or ideological 'brainwashing'.

Responsibility for overblown egotism does not lie solely or even mainly with individuals or families. If the Mighty I kind of behaviour is condoned, encouraged or even worshipped, usually because it is linked with large pay packets, then families and the brain can be said to have done their work of adapting a child to fit into its social environment, even if the cost is stunted development.

However, if a child is told and shown that he is not the centre of the universe, but rather a very much loved part of a bigger whole, then his infantile illusion of omnipotence begins to diminish, and the Gut Brain finally hands over control to the head brain.

Then the socialising Right Side of the New Brain can play its central role in the next stage of life. If this is been well handled, the ego can later fulfil its proper role and lead a teenager across the bridge from the security of the family into the unknown, to face the challenges in the outside world. This avoids encouraging the fast-track rat run by taking a more circuitous route via the Right Side of the New Brain. It is also follows the pattern of human brain development throughout history, until recently.

YOUNG PEOPLE

Whenever we look at how children develop, and in particular at anti-social behaviour in young people, it is really important to remember that children and adults do not think alike. Children's brains are still developing and they use different parts at different levels that are age and stage appropriate. Children have to begin by adapting their behaviour to those of others, not the other way round. This is, or should be, the role of the family. When it is neglected, teachers have to try to fill the gap as we have seen, which means they cannot do their real work of teaching properly.

In the *Pampered Child Syndrome*, Maggie Mamen illustrates how differently children and adults think, and how even well-meaning adult ideas can be turned upside down by children's naturally self-centred way of thinking.

For example something nearly all parents say is, "We want our children to be happy and comfortable". Many children (and some parents) interpret this to mean, "I, the child, should ALWAYS be happy and comfortable. When I experience loss or failure or feel sad, upset or disappointed, SOMEONE should make me better'". This response is age appropriate thinking for babies, but in order to progress as people, children have to learn that being happy and comfortable does not mean they get everything they want when they want it. It is a lesson not all adults have learned.

Learning to lose is critical to learning from one's mistakes, which means experiencing the emotion of grief. This is why effort needs to be praised rather than attempting to build self-esteem by ignoring mistakes, which only adds more emotional energy to the Underground Pit, while denying the Forebrain the opportunity to release feel-good chemicals when a goal is finally achieved, the basis for a realistic sense of self-worth.

Rather than taking the fast-track rat run, some young people can be blocked in the Right Side from moving on. The stage from 'one of us' to 'I' is more difficult if parents are not independent economically or psychologically, as it makes it harder for adolescents to cross that bridge. There is no path to independence for them to follow, and they find that leaving the safety of the group is too threatening. Some young people deal with that by joining a gang, which gives them independence from the family without having to face the fear of standing alone. In addition, if the only reason they are given for crossing that bridge is to earn money, which they receive anyway through social security or possibly theft, then that does not balance out what they will be leaving behind and on which they depend: the survival mechanism of group security. Of course, there are some who find the strength to break free from this pattern, often because they had someone or something beyond the family that helped them find the way across that bridge.

So what is it that children and young people need?

Role of Parents

Sue Palmer in *Toxic Childhood* is very clear that, "The needs of a small human being are much the same as they ever were: physical nurturing, nourishing food, plenty of exercise and play, adequate sleep. They need emotional and social support, which means time, attention, communication and love from those closest to them. As they get older, they must widen their social circle and learn cognitive skills. And throughout childhood, they need moral guidance. My research suggests that children's development in every one of these areas is threatened by the side effects of technological and cultural changes."

Children also need to have trust in adults' ability to deal with life's problems and crises, just as adults need leaders they can trust to make good decisions on their behalf. Otherwise there is anxiety, insecurity and a feeling of being let down. Sue Palmer recommends that, "As a society, we need to engage in ongoing discussions about the ways scientific and technological advances, which are fine for full-grown adults, may present dangers for growing children". TV programmes like *Supernanny* offer help to young children and their families by showing how children need to learn the basic rules of social behaviour, and also that parents need to learn how to apply them appropriately without the fear of 'not being liked' that has so much power in our society.

Role of Forebrain

However, a parent cannot put older children on the 'naughty step' (a *Supernanny* recommendations for inappropriate behaviour) while just talking about the consequences of unprotected sex or drinking can be ineffective. Sometimes the words literally do not 'go in', because the Forebrain that deals with consequences is not fully developed until adulthood, which is why other adults need to fill this role on behalf of young people, letting go gradually as they mature. Again this means, "Time, attention, communication and love from those closest to them".

In a world dominated by money, the different reward system that these interpersonal contacts represent is often neglected. In Integrated Thinking, the values placed on these reward systems would be rebalanced, so that the system that encourages people to grow as human beings would take precedence over the supporting role of money and the things it can buy.

Role of Fathers

In a culture where fathers are immersed in their careers or missing from their children's lives, there may be no one to help boys cross that bridge. Nor are there many places where boys learn about the world of men, and how male energy is disciplined. In the past, this was the culture of the chivalrous knight, more recently it was the role of cadet forces, scouts or youth clubs. As Sue Palmer points out in *Toxic Childhood*, "Sadly, our confused society not only fails to celebrate the masculine virtues of honour and courage, we also allow media and marketing gurus to celebrate their most ignoble impulses."

David Lammy, writing after the 2011 riots in his book *Out Of The Ashes*, raises the issue that, "Boys and young men are struggling to find their place in society. We must start to ask why. 91% of those arrested during the riots were male. Boys in young offenders' institutions have usually grown up without positive male role models, adopting the warped version of the alpha male where 'respect' is everything. They want the baggy jeans, the bling and the women from the grime videos. Carry a knife or gun, and you are a real man. Become a 'babyfather', have children with a string of different women, and people will look up to you. No one ever taught these boys that to delay gratification, the obsession with status symbols and a worldview centred on the self are markers not of manhood but of immaturity". But aren't these 'immature markers' central to perpetuating a consumer society based on the narcissistic, short term, 'greed is good' rat-run way of thinking of "I, now, more"?

Abuse

Yet it is not only boys that are affected by a society where 'personal choice' has become another word for neglect. "Dozens of cases of child prostitution and grooming of young girls by gangs of older men (for example in Rochdale) have come to light. At the heart of them, it now appears, is the ludicrous notion that children are making lifestyle 'choices' to be sexually abused or work as prostitutes", commented Joan Smith in the 'i' newspaper', 28 September 2012.

Abuse follows a predictable pattern. First there is the 'grooming', a softening up process of those in a vulnerable position so that their emotional boundaries are blurred or dropped, helped by the use of drink or drugs; they are made to feel special and the trust response is activated. Then small steps of violence, if tolerated, are increased so that the brain habituates to the abuse, until an individual's sense of identity and self-worth become dependent on doing the abuser's will. Into this broken Emotional Wheel, the abuser can then pour the contents of his own toxic Underground Pit, as he projects his inner world onto his victim, as later others do too.

Alcohol

Alcohol plays a significant role in anti-social behaviour in young people. Not only is it said to be a key factor in nearly 50% of violent crime, but also teenage brains get a bigger kick out of alcohol than adults' brains. Alcohol can cause damage to developing brains as it does to developing foetuses, and makes it harder for the Forebrain to mature.

We have seen that young people have to cross a mental and emotional bridge to leave the family circle and make their own way in the world. It could also be thought of as the bridge of a ship. On it stands the brain's captain, integrating all the information from the different parts and trying to keep on course. If distracted by sex, drink and overblown egotism, it can lead to a shipwreck, with lives lost. There are examples of this in the real world that can help us visualise its impact inside our heads.

With alcohol, brain connections break down and the Forebrain breaks away into the world of fantasy. Someone who is drunk can feel all-powerful as in babyhood, but is actually out of touch with reality. Next the skills that took years to learn, like speaking, walking, self-control can go in hours, as the infantile Primal Brain takes over. Then the lid comes off the Underground Pit to release the blocked energy in destruction and damage.

Use Your Head!

Is there a better way we, as a society, can help young people without relying so heavily on warnings of consequences?

One way might be for adults to use their own Forebrains and imagination more to get messages across. Earlier I used imagery to visualise the four parts of the brain as being like the gears of a car. There was a song in the 50's about a guy speeding up the motorway in a Bubble Car, which was a one-person covered scooter, and it was overtaking everything on the road. The punch line was he was stuck in first gear.

Many people feel they are stuck in first gear, behaving like automatons on autopilot with the Primal Brain at the wheel, wearing out the overused gear and missing out on the incredible potential of the human powerhouse, the brain. This is an image that I think young people could respond to. What would an adolescent prefer: a brain that operates like a one-speed mobility scooter or an all-terrain rugged car, ready to meet life's challenges? I suspect, however, that a sports car would be the vehicle of choice for many young people - and not so young too.

RENEWAL

Sports cars for men having a midlife crisis have become a cliché, yet beyond the symbol lies a deeper meaning, which is that this period of life is about going back to recapture parts of ourselves left behind in our youth, some with anti-social tendencies, and re-integrate them into the whole.

Midlife is the opportunity to explore paths previously overlooked or neglected, before changing direction and focus. Going back to complete unfinished business from earlier psychological stages can seem like going into reverse, causing a prolonged depression, collapse or even anti-social behaviour, when some long term brain connections begin to disintegrate. The collapse of the ego in midlife can be likened to the collapse of empire. Britain is still recovering from the loss of its empire and if not quite rising like a Phoenix from the ashes, it is at least discovering it continues to have an important if not dominant role to play in the world. Other more recent collapses include the break up of the USSR, the threat of collapse of the Eurozone or the question of Scotland's future role in the United Kingdom.

It is not just in personal and political development that collapse can be the prelude to a new way of thinking and behaving: the near collapse of the banking system and the following recession also offered the opportunity to re-think and re-focus direction. This view offers a more positive approach to the increasing role of some forms of anti-social behaviour, driven by the Primal Brain - that it can be a prelude to a change in our thinking.

The purpose of this change in direction and focus is for the Forebrain of wisdom and foresight to play a greater role, in particular to increase its regulation over the lower drives of the Gut Brain and Primal Brain. And the change does not have to stop there. By tradition, the Forebrain's third eye is a door into a higher level of consciousness, where the emotional energy is once again twisted, but this time in the opposite direction from the Underground Pit. Here, in the heavens above the Tree of Life, there is love for our enemies instead of anger; in place of fear, there is only trust, and instead of tears there is hope.

Ervin Laslo in *You Can Change The World* writes that, "Taking part in today's quiet 'consciousness revolution' calls for a different kind of growth: not growth in power and money but in wholeness, awareness and inner growth".

How can we, as a society, renew its systems and structures so that they reflect this other world, rather than the Underground Pit accessed via the Serpent's trapdoor? I think that before we can reach this level, we first need individually and collectively to have made better use of the brain's integrating function, the Crossing Bridge or *corpus callosum.*

CROSSROADS FOR SOCIETY

I have spoken about the Crossing Bridge many times, as a symbolic image or as a device for developing greater awareness rather than as an actual physical reality, but sometimes instead of bringing clarity, it can cause confusion. This is because people use it in differing ways at different stages of life. Some will be crossing it tentatively for the first time at two years old, or more strongly at adolescence; others will be crossing it when they join the world of work outside the family home, others in midlife. Some will be going back to help others across.

Part of the new way of thinking is that instead of having opposing sides, crossing the bridge is a two-way process, seeing the other side's point of view, learning what life is like on the other side of that bridge - like young people learning what life is like on the other side of the world, or people in power learning to live without it, politicians learning what it is like to be unemployed, men learning to care for others, women to be the family breadwinner.

The new way of thinking, Integrated Thinking, integrates the personal stages of development with social and political developmental stages, to show how changes in our present way of thinking could benefit individuals and society as a whole. However, information about the disadvantages of a particular way of thinking and the benefits to be gained by changing to a new, more integrated way of thinking are not enough for change to happen. Like decision-making and the political process, we need to engage the emotions and the will. We also need to respond to change personally and to be able to relate it to our own lives. In particular, we need to make greater use of the Forebrain and its control over the Primal Brain of habit.

In order to do this, I would suggest that we link the kind of changes we are facing at this crossroads in Western society with the changes faced by individuals at the crossroads stage during midlife. In midlife, we too can choose whether to try desperately to stay young, as the emphasis seems to be in society today, or grow into maturity with good grace; we can choose whether to continue to seek growth in money, power and possessions, or to cut back on our material demands; to continue drawing on finite energy supplies or conserve them while growing in a new way. These are some of the similar challenges facing society today.

And we can return to the dreams and ideals of youth when we believed we could change the world in the 60's, incorporating them into the body of experience we have built up as we mature.

Just as an individual can choose whether to integrate the two sides of the New Brain or to keep up the old divisions, so as a society we can ask whether we continue the opposing sides of the great political divide, or start to work together to find common ground. We can continue to blame others for our social problems, or we can look at how we have contributed to them, using our empathy to see life as others see it.

Using the framework of human development, we can also see the forces that might be holding us back. And to ask who are the people most suited to help us through, those who created and misused the present systems to their own advantage, or those who bring a more caring, sharing and balanced integrity?

There are no easy answers, but if we tap into the brain's vast potential and integrate it with higher levels of human development, we can do it. We will be looking at these higher levels of human development and their role later, in Section 4.

SECTION REVIEW

We have been looking in Section 2 at how the stages of social and political development can be integrated into a new way of thinking based on brain development. In Chapter 5, we looked at why our present ways of thinking are often conflicting and contradictory, their effect on society and why we need to make greater use of the brain's integrating function. By linking political development within the same framework, we saw in Chapter 6 how changes in our thinking could be reflected in the world of politics and law-enforcement. Chapter 7 looked at what could be holding us back from social change, and the links between the human unconscious and the criminal underworld. In the final chapter of Section 2, we saw how anti-social behaviour can give us clues as to what is going wrong in society, and how we are now faced with a choice and change of focus and direction, as in midlife.

Before we move on to Section 3, I want to clarify what I mean by the interconnectedness or 'mirroring' between the brain and the outside world. Just as 'equal' is different from 'same', so integrating inside and out does not mean they are identical. That way madness lies. There has to be a boundary between what is in our heads and the real world, which means becoming more aware of our unseen processes, part of the purpose of Integrated Thinking. And the bigger the stage, the more important is this distinction between inside and out.

In Section 3, we will look at how the human development framework is mirrored in the wider world as the next stage towards Integrated Thinking. We will also consider whose way of thinking needs to change.

SECTION 3

GLOBAL DEVELOPMENT

"The brain is - in fact has to be - a metaphor for the world".
Iain McGilchrist

INTRODUCTION

We begin this Section by looking back to see how far we have come in integrating human brain development with the outside world, and how this could support change. At the beginning of the book, I proposed that before changing the way that people think, we needed to be clear about what was meant by 'our present way of thinking'.

In Section 1, I showed that there are in fact many different ways of thinking, which are linked to the stages of brain development. By integrating these different parts into a new framework, I outlined a way of thinking which I call Integrated Thinking. In Section 2, I took this integrating process a step further by linking the framework for the brain with social and political development, since it seems that the brain repeats the pattern of its own development in the systems and structures it creates in the world outside.

This highlighted the need for change because conflicts between the different parts of the brain are mirrored in the social and political worlds, which results in less flexibility to respond to new challenges. It became clear during these explorations that over-stimulation of the Serpent and the Primal Brain made change, integration and the roles of the Crossing Bridge and Forebrain more difficult.

Many of the challenges nations face politically and socially arise from the wider world, so in Section 3 we will extend this process of integration onto the global stage. In Chapter 9 we will be looking at global history and some of the present crises in the world through the framework of brain development. Chapter 10 looks at recent conflicts in the West and in developing countries, including conflicts about energy, and how we can bridge the gap and bring the different sides closer together.

In Chapter 11 we consider the limits of the Old IT, Information Technology, in a review of the global Internet network and its effect on the human brain, and also consider what could happen if the dominant way of thinking collapses. Chapter 12 will try to predict how a new world order could arise from disorder when walls come down and leading players change positions, and while the Middle East and Eurozone are also undergoing upheavals.

This brief review of global development and its place within Integrated Thinking will also help address the question of who needs to change, and who could guide us to a more positive and productive future.

9 WORLD IN CRISIS

In Section 3 we will be taking Integrated Thinking a step further by linking personal and global development. This chapter begins by revisiting history through the New IT framework or model of the stages of brain development outlined in Section 1. Each person's life on earth is his or her own story, while mankind's collective life on earth is called history. According to the historian Simon Schama, "History is an adventure in self-recognition, a way to see ourselves in the mirror of time".

Later in this chapter, we will use the same model to look at the challenges that are presented today by the environmental crisis, the economic crisis and the crisis in confidence in our institutions.

HISTORY

Today we can see that in both the human brain and the outside world there are different parts at differing stages of development, each playing a vital role, but often in conflict. It is also clear that many parts of the brain and the world today are neglected, exhausted or polluted. Some would say this similarity was a co-incidence, and it is certainly a very useful analogy, but Integrated Thinking would suggest a deeper link between stages of brain development and mankind's history, that the one is a mirror of the other. Iain McGilchrist in *The Master and the Emissary* describes the brain as being, "Something like a huge country, as a nested structure of villages and towns, gathered into counties, regions and even partly autonomous states".

Nations and empires have their own cycle of growth and decline over time, similar to the stages in brain development, and this similarity extends to other areas. In *The Quest For Identity In 21st Century*, Susan Greenfield provides very detailed lists of the similarities between neurons in the brain and people; between brains and societies, and between the development of personal identity and the development of organisations - a strong indication of how the brain repeats its own pattern.

We saw that the first part of the brain to develop in a baby and in mankind itself was the Primal Brain, which lies behind the mouth. Throughout history, the Serpent's world has been ruled by the competitive law of the jungle, reflected today in the image of Man the Hunter or the dog-eat-dog survival skills in the urban jungle, whereas the Emotional Wheel is more associated with the gatherers and travelling tribes who often form enclosing circles for protection, and remain close to the rhythms of the natural world.

On mankind's journey, people learned to walk on two feet, feed themselves by their own efforts rather than taking just what was naturally provided, and how to live in societies as they left the jungle behind. So man moved from Africa, home of his birth and settled in other parts of the world. The East developed faster than the West in early global history, just as the Right Side developed first in the brain. As Iain McGilchrist notes, "In general, the [Right Side] matures first [and] the Oriental experience of the world is still effectively grounded in that of the [Right Side]".

He follows the mirroring of brain development mainly through European history, showing the eventual dominance of the Left Side of the New Brain. He begins with Ancient Greece, when writing first changed direction, followed by the Roman straight lines that replaced stone circles, and the late Roman period of global ambition, representing an attempt by the Left Side to "go it alone". Then came the latency period of the Dark Ages, which in human development usually covers the period between 7 and 11 years of age. To kick-start the idealism of the Renaissance in the Middle Ages, the West often made often unacknowledged use of the work of Muslim scholars, built on the knowledge from earlier civilisations, in just the same way that the Left Side can sometimes make unacknowledged use of the Right Side's gifts and knowledge.

The age of exploration and enlightenment followed, reminiscent of the adolescence stage of development, leading up to Age of Industry. Iain McGilchrist writes that, "There became evident a gradual shift of emphasis from [Right Side] to Left, in which a more atomistic individuality characterised by ambition and competitiveness becomes more salient. It is notable that when the [Left Side] takes a step forward, it does so in a manner which is absolute and intolerant, and sweeps opposition aside: the Reformation, the Cromwellian Revolution, the French Revolution, the rise of scientific materialism, the Industrial Revolution."

However throughout history, following an extreme positioning by the Left Side, there has been the counterbalancing swing back to greater tolerance and nature, such as the Romantic or Pre-Raphaelite Movements.

Iain McGilchrist then goes on to consider a very real possibility. "What if the [Left Side] were able to externalise its own workings? I would contend that a combination of urban environments which are increasingly rectilinear grids of machine-made surfaces, an unprecedented assault on the natural world, the omnipresence of television and the Internet, have between them created a replica of life as processed by the [Left Side]."

He then asks what the world would look like if the Left Side became so dominant, it managed to suppress the Right Side's world altogether and the world became exclusively Left Brain. If this happened, he says he would expect to see an increase in people and the natural world being seen as mere 'things'; the world would become more virtualised with numbers replacing individuals, and that there would be an increase in the lack of trust.

How far away from that world are we today? I will try to answer that question by looking at the elements of his apocalyptic vision: first we will consider the environmental crisis in nature; then look at the economic crisis and how figures have become so important, and finally think about the lack of trust in the crisis of confidence. Whether the world is becoming more virtualised is the subject of Chapter 11.

ENVIRONMENTAL CRISIS

So, how far has the Left Side's worldview affected the way we see people and nature? Economic thinking tends to view people and the natural world as 'things', but for many, it is the Right Side's connections and cycles that more accurately describe the relationship between people and nature.

Just as a baby inherits many of his basic brain structures and information from his mother, so people have inherited much from nature's systems. Human brains and ecology are based on the similar principles of networks, flow, cycles and using 'nested' systems where each new system is built around an earlier one, like Russian dolls. Furthermore, both the brain and the land can be 'over-farmed', some parts overloaded, others neglected and their recycling processes misused, with potentially damaging chemicals being used to keep output high. Is deforestation a mirror image of Alzheimer's disease, when the natural pruning of the brain's branches reaches a non-sustainable level?

Although no longer seeing nature as a thing to be controlled and plundered, over-emotional connectivity can go too far in the misguided talk about people saving the planet. The earth does not need people to save her; it can survive without us as it has always done. It is our survival that is at risk. A similar change in thinking happens in early childhood when a baby first thinks he controls his mother so that she serves his needs, nourishes him and takes away waste. He then realises that he is in fact totally dependent on her. His whole perspective of himself - and his mother - has to change, and this takes time and can be quite disturbing.

The next stage in this re-visioning process in the brain was called 'guilt and reparation' by the psychoanalyst Melanie Klein, when older babies realise they have taken from their mothers without thought or care, feel guilty about it and want to put right the damage they believe they have caused. However, this can lead to an egocentric belief called infantile omnipotence when a baby thinks that saving his mother is all down to him. This belief reappears in the scripts for many rescue myths such as St George and the Dragon or the Crusaders rescuing the holy city of Jerusalem, and seems to have been re-awakened in the environmental movement mission to 'save the planet'.

Over-emotional identification can be misleading, for the reality is that the fantasy rescue mission in a baby totally underestimates a mother's powers of regeneration and ability to take care of herself, and so it is with the 'save the earth' rescue mission. We need to separate inner fantasy from outside reality, which is why I emphasise that integration does not mean that inside and out are identical, and why it is important to balance thinking from both Sides of the New Brain to include Left Side detachment skills.

Many would wish to separate, too, the idea of a close connection between women and 'mother nature' or 'mother earth'. However, the idea of the earth being like a female body can be used as an analogy or metaphor in order to create an image to help us understand more clearly what is happening on the earth today.

Many scientists now accept that the earth is an animate body, a self-regulating, living system they call Gaia. If that is true, what stage of development has Gaia reached? A Greenpeace leaflet in 1989 suggested the idea of midlife: "Planet earth is 4,600 million years old. If we condense this inconceivable time-span into an understandable concept, we can liken earth to a person of 46 years old".

For most people, midlife is about change, often unexpected, sometimes unwelcome. Women usually reach their midlife earlier than men, just as nature's systems reached the so-called 'tipping point' before the cracks began to appear in the man-made world in the banking crisis of 2008. The female menopause is sometimes called the 'climacteric' or The Change, a time of unpredictable mood and temperature swings, hot flushes and flooding. Temperature swings, hot flashes and flooding are the symptoms that the earth is showing now in climate change. "Since we, as women, are one with the earth, is our massive collective change her change as well?" asks Susun Weed in *The New Menopause Years*.

Other similarities between environmental change and The Change include being past the peak of energy production, and the need to spend the remaining energy more wisely and find new sources, particularly those that do not come from underground.

Recycling and adaptive systems are overstretched at both the personal and global level, and both stages of development depend less on material growth and more on personal growth and concern for the future.

Some of the symptoms of women's climacteric change occur naturally, others are as a result of their own actions - again like the earth. The physical changes of menopause bring psychological and personal changes too. Women in midlife, once children had left home, often moved from their traditional role of caring for others and the security of the family group to find independence and individuality in the marketplace, to start new careers or find they enjoy running voluntary committees.

Now this kind of personal change is not only political, it is global too, as women move into the global market place, take up new careers, run organisations and nations worldwide. Many men, when experiencing their own midlife stage, are passing women travelling in the opposite direction. This rebalancing between masculine and feminine hormones in both men and women is reflected in what is seen as the 'feminising' of many areas of life, even affecting men's sperm count.

As their feminine hormone levels decrease, women's masculine hormones help integrate their multi-tasking abilities with more self-focused, assertive skills, so women make more balanced decisions, which could have an effect on developing Integrated Thinking and decision-making on a global scale.

I see the difference between the environmental position proposed by some and the increasing role of women in the world almost as a re-run of the 1960's, now that particular generation is in their sixties or older. "Why do the sixties seem to matter so much? The truth is we have never really left the sixties", according to Andrew Marr in his book *A History Of Modern Britain*. In the 1960's and 70's, there was the hippie movement and communal living close to the earth, claiming 'all you need is love', yet it was those in the Women's Movement that made the real changes, personal, political and legal.

Now we have the green environmentalists, focusing on community and the planet, and we need a new Women's Movement of 'silver radicals' who want to revisit and complete the work they started in the 60's, particularly when they consider the unforeseen consequences of changes they helped set in motion, especially for young women today.

ECONOMIC CRISIS

The second element in Iain McGilchrist's vision of an all-dominant Left Side of the New Brain replicating itself in the world outside was one, "Where numbers would replace individuals". In the world of economics, it sometimes seems as if numbers have almost become more important than people. The market is sometimes described in semi-religious terms, 'an invisible hand', while people and nature are seen as 'things' in a big machine for making money. After the collapse of communism, capitalism looked like the only game in town, and some in the financial markets played it like a game, ignoring risk and consequences until the markets too came close to collapse.

"Capitalism is the least worst way to run an economy", claims Edmund Conway in *50 Economic Ideas You Really Need to Know*. "The money markets are the central nervous system of the world's financial system ... and measuring how much money is flowing round an economy is one of the key ways to determine that economy's health." It is clear that the economy is struggling to cope, like a body under stress.

John Lanchester in his book *Whoops* sees the economic crisis as evidence of poor health, with the credit crunch as a small heart attack, perhaps due to over-consumption. He says that we have to make sure it does not happen again, otherwise, "We'll be doing the equivalent of discharging ourselves from hospital after that heart attack, and going straight out to celebrate with cigarettes, Tequila and a Big Mac". I knew a man once who did just that, and he had an even bigger collapse later, after which he finally turned his life around.

The economic crisis has led to an age of austerity, with personal and public downsizing affecting many aspects of life. Downsizing and the related concept of a global power-down are difficult for some to adapt to, but perhaps is easier for others. There is one group of people who have already cut back in response to having less to spend, but who nevertheless realise that there are other types of growth, not merely material or economic growth. In economic terms, they are called 'grey power'; in personal development terms, they are those who have survived another crisis - that midlife crisis again.

Economic growth was founded on the belief that things could only get bigger and better, like house prices, market confidence, wage rises and so on. In both personal and economic crises, reality breaks through with the loss of those unrealistic beliefs. In midlife, it is possible to appreciate that small is beautiful and that bigger is not necessarily better, and that includes unregulated over-consumption and unrealistic lifestyles that helped fuel the economic crisis and expanding waistlines.

Midlife is also a time when one faces death, and it is possible to detect similarities between the way that people are responding to the global economic crisis and the way they respond emotionally to the prospect of death, described in more detail in Chapter 5.

Many still reject the new information about the need to change and are in denial, and some are carrying on expecting to receive big bonuses or wanting more deregulation. They are not ready to let go their 'might-have-beens' in the kind of life they thought and expected to have. "Just tighten our belts for a while, and then we'll get back to normality and economic growth", seems to be the present attitude of some who deny reality. Others are fearful for the future, and feel helpless to counter the negativity and conflict that seem to dominate the news.

Then comes the true reckoning of loss, when compassion helps those still clinging to the past to move into acceptance and to let go what is no longer needed mentally and emotionally while retaining the best for the future. Television makeover programmes do something similar with hoarders' possessions.

The pursuit of money, power and possessions no longer seems so appropriate in an age of austerity, and there are signs that the obsession with the pursuit of youth that has so dominated many aspects of modern life (and many at midlife) is finally giving way to a more mature approach. This is consistent with Integrated Thinking that seeks to increase the role of the Forebrain, rewired in midlife in preparation for the more mature stage of development.

Christine Lagarde, head of IMF, speaking at the US State Department in 2012 said that, "Global economic leaders now need to take a more holistic approach". Hannah Rosin in *The End Of Men* sees this more holistic [or integrated] approach as linked to the role of women in economic terms. "When economists assess a country's future, they see ambivalence over women's role as the critical factor blocking its progress".

One generally accepted aspect of the global economic crisis is that the regulators failed in their oversight role. This is similar to the situation where the Forebrain fails to oversee lower levels. This lack of regulatory oversight has affected other institutions too, such as the media, which is contributing to the crisis in confidence.

CRISIS OF CONFIDENCE

We are looking at Iain McGilchrist's vision in *The Master And The Emissary* of a world where an exclusive Left Side of the New Brain has been replicated in the world outside, which he predicted would lead to an "increase in the lack of trust". It is true that today there seems to be a general loss of confidence in the man-made world to provide that secure foundation. The institutions and people we used to depend on, such as banks, politicians, the media - even the police and the BBC - no longer seem so worthy of our trust.

This sense of a loss of certainty is typical of midlife. We start to understand that we are all only human, we all make mistakes, and that people are mostly trying to do the best they can with what they have. We no longer look to them 'out there' to make everything right, realising it is up to us too. And we start to look for something more, something we can put our trust in. This could be the ability of people to adapt to and create change, for this is what has ensured our survival so far.

It is not just trust in the systems that has been damaged, it is also the loss of trust in our present way of thinking to solve these problems. In David Smith's view in *The Age Of Instability*, "We should not forget the potentially long-lasting consequences of the erosion of trust in such basic parameters of the market system as the sanctity of contracts and property rights, the rule of law, and the robustness of the capital structure. Not surprisingly, given the extent of the gains that were privatised and the losses that are now being socialised, the demise is occurring in the context of popular anger and confusion."

Only in the environment crisis are there signs that Ian McGilchrist's three predictions for an exclusive Left Brain world are being seriously challenged. We cannot blame the brain: it has adapted us to fit into the society that a dominant but not yet exclusive Left Side of the New Brain has created. Iain McGilchrist again: "The [Left Side] takes a single solution that best fits what it already knows. The [Right Side] is more capable of a frame shift. It presents an array of possible solutions". The Right Side deals with uncertainty better than the Left Side. Midlife is also a time of uncertainty and instability, but one of its aims is to balance the two Sides and use whichever is most appropriate in a given situation. These aims are also central to Integrated Thinking.

Also critical is the redirecting of the Primal Brain drives through greater Forebrain maturity. There have been times in earth's history when the north and south poles have reversed. What if that happened inside our brains so that the Primal Brain, dominant in a consumer society, and the Forebrain reversed their positions of importance in our lives?

Those in midlife with well-developed Forebrains have the experience to know what works in practice, and want to pass this knowledge onto others. Al Gore in *The Earth In Balance* says that, "Erik Erikson was the first to document the development stages of life that all of us experience. Midlife is the stage when 'generativity' is the central focus: one focuses on being fruitful for the future." It could be called a legacy, a word heard often in the context of the London Olympic Games 2012, while fruitfulness depends on pruning, whether the pruning of fruit crops or the brain pruning that happens as part of the process of change.

We are all now on that bridge of change, we are all in this together, on which even the Keynesian theory of economics depends. Integrated Thinking sees political, social and global change through the framework of stages in brain development, which offers a new way of thinking about change that is personal and positive, and hopefully will avoid the kind of world Iain McGilchrist envisaged.

CHAPTER REVIEW

In this chapter, we have looked at some global issues through the framework of human development, with reference to history and present economic and environmental crises, and also the crisis of confidence; we will come back to trust in Section 4.

In asking the question of what and who needs to change, the dominance of the Left Side of the New Brain is a prime candidate. This could lead us to suppose that those who would like to see the collapse of capitalism and Big Bad Business are on the right track, but it may be that their emphasis on community indicates that they themselves have yet to cross the bridge into Left Side individuality. An idealistic belief that the collapse of capitalism would lead to a return to a simpler, more localised and more natural way of life may be unrealistic, for any kind of collapse can also release the contents of the Underground Pit. It is to the role of the collective unconscious on a global scale that we now turn.

10 CONFLICT

I have been using the model of Integrated Thinking to link some of today's global crises with the stages in brain development. Crises reveal cracks in individual, social and global mental constructs and create conflicts that have to be resolved. Global conflicts can be between nations, between different belief constructs or about energy supplies, and some conflicts can contain all these elements.

The unconscious makes use of these cracks to do its work as an opening of the trapdoor, and its role has to be integrated into the bigger picture of a new way of thinking, while at the same time drawing a distinction between the unconscious' world of inner fantasy and outer reality.

GLOBAL STAGE

The unconscious has many automated programmes under the control of the Serpent's autopilot that can bypass rational argument, facts and common sense, like those caught up in its virtual world. It causes conflict between our inner drives and the words we use to justify our actions. Within its limited thinking, the unconscious is right, it does have a job to do, and in midlife one of these is to complete developmental tasks unfinished from earlier stages.

In the story of life, each of us has many roles to play, and we all project inner dramas onto the outside world, usually unconsciously, choosing people to play roles in our inner script to enable us to 'act out' or re-live earlier conflicts and hopefully release them. In order to separate from the family and develop his own individual ego identity, a teenage boy's key task during adolescence is to overtake or overthrow his father 'to become a man'. Some cultures have rites of passage for this stage of separation, but if a boy cannot do this at the right time, perhaps because his father is too powerful (like President Bush Snr) or because his father is too ill after a stroke (like Mr Blair Snr), then the developmental task can resurface later.

Rupert Cornwell asked in the *Independent on Sunday*, 22 February 2006, "Why was Bush Jnr bent on war with Iraq almost from his first day in office?" The answer in his view was that, "The son is locked in his oedipal struggle with the father, whose achievements for so long eclipsed his own". And Oliver James in *Affluenza* goes further: "The reason why children do not rebel against an inescapable family system is fear. They deal with it by feeling intense hostility towards despised others. This explains George Bush's passionate desire to rid the world of evil: the real darkness in his life was his ... perfect father".

It seems that, instead of just being personal, this inner drama can be projected outwards onto the global stage by world leaders. If the inner and outer worlds are not separated, there is a very clear and present danger to us all, as in the Iraq War. Enter Saddam Hussein, perfect in the role of the 'Big Bad Daddy' whom Tony Blair and George W Bush believed they just had to overtake and overthrow.

If there is a real baddy in the story, it is the unconscious, although as we have seen, its role has sometimes been misunderstood. The unconscious usually operates unseen, like the underworld, and it can hijack our thinking for its own purposes, just as terrorists can hijack planes. It does not have the ability to foresee the consequences of its actions; it just makes sure a man does what a man has to do, as the saying goes.

In the world of myth, getting hold of a father's energy source is essential to a young man's phallic dominance which may explain why getting hold of those hidden weapons (and oil supplies) played such a critical role in the unfolding drama of the Iraq War.

What has been the effect on ordinary Iraqis, as the supposed beneficiaries of this drama? According to Patrick Cockburn in the *'i'* newspaper on 4 March 2013, "The US and the UK have sought to play down overwhelming evidence that their invasion and occupation has produced one of the most dysfunctional and crooked governments in the world. The record of failure, given the financial resources available, is astounding. Iraq is disintegrating under mounting political, social and economic crises, say its leaders ... even though Iraq now enjoys £66bn a year in oil revenues".

For the central actors in the drama in 2003, challenging and supplanting a dictator may have completed personal unfinished business - 'mission accomplished' - but it could also have offered a thwarted actor his biggest role yet. In the drama acted out on the world stage called the Iraq War, people can understand why President Bush might have wanted to outgun his father, but why, they ask, was Prime Minister Blair such a willing sidekick? Perhaps overthrowing Saddam Hussein did more than complete an unfinished psychological task; maybe it also allowed Tony Blair to play his favourite role on the world stage, that of Saviour.

Did this messianic self-image begin when, in his own eyes at least, the young Tony stepped centre stage to 'save the family' after his father's stroke to became the 'man of the family'? Later he stepped into John Smith's shoes to 'save' the Labour Party, then came rescuing Britain from conservatism, next was Africa, even the world. Anthony Seldon in *Blair Unbound* tells how, "Hubris came to the fore. He had transformed the Labour Party: surely transforming the country and creating a New Britain would not be too difficult. One senior official said: 'Tony Blair is now in la-la-land: he wants to sort out Israel, Iraq, Afghanistan, global warming, poverty ....'".

In Chapter 9 we looked at how this rescue fantasy can arise in babyhood and may be applied to many rescue missions, including saving the planet. Here it seems likely it was applied in the man-made world.

Tony Blair was right about many things: there is a struggle going on between opposing forces; the Middle East is the main battleground and we do need a new way. Yet the question has to be asked - who was writing his script and who were the fellow actors in the drama, feeding him his lines? One voice in the unconscious tells us we are always right, massaging our egos, like a smooth-talking spindoctor. Peter Mandelson would be perfect in the role. But behind the image lies the one who really drives the action, the angry one who represents the parts the sainted one cannot reveal. Now why does that make me think of Alastair Campbell? In Tony Blair's own words in *Tony Blair: A Journey*, "I was never totally sure whether Gordon Brown really did buy the illusion that I was just a front-man, carefully tutored by Peter Mandelson and then by Alastair Campbell".

In the unconscious there are many characters and many voices, but there is another quieter voice that tells a different story. The Forebrain's conscience tells us when we are wrong, when we need to say 'sorry', and when it is time for the overdeveloped ego to leave the stage, his cover finally blown when the mask of self-righteousness falls.

DEVELOPING COUNTRIES

As we have seen, the brain is made up of different parts at differing stages of development that are often in conflict. Psychologists call this inner discord 'cognitive dissonance'; in relationships we call it arguments or family break down, and in the world outside, we call it hostilities or war.

Different parts at differing stages also reflect the way nations work, some we call developed, others as developing or Third World countries. We can see reflected in the West's history the stages that developing countries are now experiencing. Europe too had its Crusades when knights were promised forgiveness and rewards in heaven; the West had its own slave trade when human supplies to the sugar trade created a rat run to economic wealth from Africa to the West, like the brain's Primal/Left Side rat run.

It is not that long ago that elections were bought, women were considered the property of their husbands, yet young women were willing to die for democracy. "The transformation of the West from feudal monarchies to democratic nation-states took time, trial and error. Today we are witnessing a new historical transformation in the former Soviet Union, Eastern Europe and countries in the Muslim world", writes John L Esposito in *The Islamic Threat*.

Mobile phones can play a positive role in developing countries, offering young people the opportunity to by-pass parental and state authority where they are blocking freedom and democracy, and by offering programmes to wipe out illiteracy, particularly for women and in rural areas. Yet we can also see how developing nations are in danger of making the same mistakes the West made, just as former colonies in their search for self-determination often seemed to repeat the mistakes of their old colonial masters.

Trying to introduce ideas of democracy, based on personal independence, into a society that is still dominated by an all-powerful 'father figure', is like giving children too much freedom before their brains are ready to handle it. Basic rules have to be in place first, those building blocks for the mental construct of independence.

One of those basic building blocks for nations is that rules are encoded, recorded and enforced, such as the rule of law and the independence of judges. Security of property registration and rights is needed, and institutions people can trust, and not the dominance of the underworld or the unconscious. In *The Rational Optimist*, Matt Ridley puts forward the example of Botswana. "Botswana's biggest advantage is one that the rest of Africa could easily have shared: good institutions. In particular, Botswana turns out to have secure, enforceable property rights that are fairly widely distributed and fairly well respected." The rule of law is very different from the unregulated freedoms of the market, but which dominates in the West today and in developing countries that seek to copy the West's way of life?

A global community needs all parts of the world to work together, just as the brain needs to integrate all the different parts, with an increased role for the world's equivalent of a global Forebrain: the United Nations. The vision of the United Nations and the European Union was to reduce conflict, but the UN is more like a wounded body torn on the cross as it tries to balance national interests with global security, and seeks to reconcile its own warring and peacekeeping roles.

In his memoirs, former United Nations secretary-general Kofi Annan came to the conclusion that the UN had to be given the mandate and the means to intervene within states as well as between them. "The United Nations has to be willing to intervene to protect not only countries that were victims of aggression from other countries, but also individuals at the hands of their own states". In a similar way, the state took time to intervene in how children were raised or in marital violence, compared with national defence.

In *The Unfinished Global Revolution*, Mark Malloch-Brown speaks of the problem of integrating the two arms of the UN, military and humanitarian intervention, and of the danger when the rules of the unregulated market fill the gap left by the absence of a global regulatory system.

More positively, Steven Pinker describes *The Better Angels Of Our Nature* as being empathy, self-control, moral sense and reason, which with the historical forces of the judiciary and democracy, commerce and feminisation, have led to a retreat from violence through the ages, from the first agricultural civilisations to the more recent periods of global peace and the rights revolutions.

He also talks of experiments that support the idea that violence arises from an imbalance between Primal Brain impulses and Forebrain self-control, which also supports the key principle of Integrated Thinking. When the Left Side dominates, information-processing can outstrip personal growth in people, and in developing nations new technologies can outstrip human rights.

ENERGY

One potential source of national and global conflict is in ensuring and protecting energy supplies for the future. If we apply the model of Integrated Thinking from personal development, we see that in the first half of life, people draw on the fuel of the unreleased store of emotional energy from earlier stages, 'fossilised' in the unconscious' Underground Pit, to drive us forward. This adrenalin-fuelled energy store includes the pain of the ignored or bullied child, the unfinished business of uncompleted developmental tasks or the over-indulgence of a golden child, habituated to the belief he deserves special treatment. It also contains things we missed out on or overdid, maybe could not deal with at the time or did not get a chance to explore.

That Underground Pit starts to overflow in midlife, as the unconscious prepares to clear out ready for the next stage of life. As the store begins to run out, the body in response extracts every bit of adrenalin to keep going, like energy companies are extracting every last bit of fossil fuel from below the earth until new sources of energy are brought online - a difficult balance. At midlife, people have passed their peak of underground energy storage, just as in the outside world the oil peak has also passed. "Most if not all OPEC members have exaggerated the size of their reserves. Whether or not OPEC reserves were hyped, whether or not the cartel's fields were nearing a **midlife crisis** (my emphasis), plenty of crude was coming out of the ground", according to Peter Maas in *Crude World*. Oil is rather like adrenalin, it smoothes the wheels of industry but not the Emotional Wheel.

Perhaps in looking at how people need to find new energy sources in midlife, the world can find it easier to let go its dependence on oil, and the damage and conflict it can cause. In *Whoops*, John Lanchester says that, "The most important ethical, political and ecological idea can be summed up in one simple word:
Enough."

Those nations that do have enough need to step back, reflect on what they are doing, what they can let go and change, how to make better use of their resources, how to appreciate different forms of capital, and so aim to model a new way for the rest of the world. But who in a 24/7 world has the time to 'stop and stare' with no day for rest, when the consumer machine has to be constantly fed and communication is unending? Yet if we did give our Primal Brain time out each week to let our Wounded Body integrate and our Forebrain reflect, we might realise that, yes, we can still grow by creating new brain connections especially in the Forebrain where creativity and wisdom lie.

One can be more energy efficient with a newly re-wired Forebrain and cut back materially and economically but continue to grow by developing and integrating all the neglected parts of oneself. The same could happen in the outside world too - to use that mirror image again.

I want here to explore the mirror concept in a little more detail, and its role in seeking to balance the inner and outer worlds. The recently discovered mirror cells in the brain allow one person to feel what they see another feeling and so help develop compassion, but mirror cells seem to be under-active in some people, as previously mentioned, or can be distorted in a few sadistic people so that they feel pleasure at seeing another in pain. Others may be unconsciously aware that something is missing and try to compensate in the outside world by using the gaze of other people as mirrors in which to see themselves reflected in egotism or narcissism, or try to compensate inner impoverishment with outer riches.

With the development of consciousness, the mind's eye becomes a two-way mirror, so we can look inside and out clearly. It is tilted upwards to reflect light from higher levels of development rather than tilted downwards to reflect the molten core of the Underground Pit's fiery furnace. The concepts of consciousness and the Mind will be explored further in Section 4.

BRIDGING THE GAP

If the brain has indeed recreated its own workings where we can see them on the outside, we can use the outside like a mirror to look back inside ourselves, and see what needs to change. We can see what happens in the outside world when one part dominates, takes over most of the resources, and leaves the rest neglected, underdeveloped or polluted, and consider that might be what we are doing to ourselves.

One of the desires of maturity is to pass on what has been learnt to help others; so it is that more developed nations want to pass on knowledge about legal and political institutions in a democracy to developing countries. As with children, it is important to know when to intervene and give aid, and when to let them find their own way.

It is not a one-way exchange between more to less developed regions: both can learn from each other. People who have overdeveloped one part will have other brain regions that are less well developed. In the same way, nations and world regions that may be less developed in Western style thinking, economics or way of living, will still have much to teach the West about building strong communities, about living with less or cultivating higher levels of awareness. Young people who travel to developing countries during their 'gap' year are literally filling in the gaps in their own development left by the dominance of the Left Side of the New Brain in the West, as they integrate their experiences into a wider framework.

Without the inner integration of internal unity, like the consent of the United Nations, there is a danger that when the inner wall falls, the unconscious will flood in. When the Berlin wall fell, in rushed the Mafia; when Baghdad fell, anarchy took over and when Middle Eastern dictators fell, in came Al Qa'ida. There was no immediate or automatic return to a more peaceful or more natural lifestyle. If Western style thinking or its economic systems collapse, we need to have something else in place that has already contained the Underground Pit into a bigger framework.

CHAPTER REVIEW

This chapter seems to indicate that we all have to change our thinking in ways that are appropriate to our time and place. We have to avoid choosing leaders who are dominated by primitive drives, and help developing countries avoid making the same mistakes as developed countries. We have to resolve conflicts over energy supplies and prevent uncontrolled forces taking over when dictators are overthrown or walls fall.

Critical to reducing personal and global conflict is to reflect on those we see as our enemies. They could be reflecting rejected or neglected aspects of ourselves that we have projected onto them, which need to be re-integrated.

We have been looking in the mirror of global events to see a reflection of the workings of our own brains; next we will look at the 'global brain' - which is how some describe the Internet. The Old IT, Information Technology, was seen as the way forward, but perhaps it is now time for it to play a supporting rather than dominant role in a new way of thinking. The virtualised world is the final element in Iain McGilchrist's vision of an exclusively Left Brain created world, where the line between reality and fantasy is blurred.

11 INTERNET

In chapter 10, we looked at some of the conflicts in the world; in this chapter, we will see how the unconscious has found its way onto the global stage. The brain would seem to recreate its own workings in the systems and structures in the outside world, and recreating the unconscious is no exception. The unconscious includes the Underground Pit that stores unused or overused parts of the human system, and is linked to the Primal Brain through the autopilot.

The new way of thinking, Integrated Thinking, is based on the stages of brain development, and one fundamental aspect of brain development is that it makes use of old parts for new purposes. Therefore, Integrated Thinking or the New IT has to incorporate the Old IT, Information Technology, into its framework, especially its role in young people's lives.

I-BRAIN

In Chapter 5, we saw how the Primal Brain seems to play a large role in modern life, and so do computers. Having mobiles, computers and TV on all the time is like having the Primal Brain constantly on alert, while swiping touch screens recalls babies pointing at what they want. John Arden in *Rewire Your Brain* talks of how, "In today's society, mobiles, Blackberries, instant messaging and mass media bombardment combine to erode our attention and memory skills. You have to resist attention being fragmented. We all have the necessary ingredients for an attention-deficit society." Fragmentation also makes integration more difficult.

Computer-Brain Link

The brain has sometimes been compared to a computer, but actually each cell within the brain is more like a super-computer. Link the billions of cells up and you have the ever-expanding networks of communication and information that make up the human brain. Link computers together and you have the world wide web, with ever-expanding networks of communication and information that make up the Internet. A *Horizon* programme in October 2006 claimed there were three mysteries: the origin of the universe, the origin of life and how the brain works. A scientist in another TV programme pointed out that, "If you think the Internet has caused a revolution, see what happens when we really understand the brain", an understanding that has really taken off since the 1980's.

We know that the brain can link up with other brains to form a single network through mirror cells and empathy in the Emotional Wheel. What has only recently been realised is that what we can do with people, we can also do with machines, particularly those machines that are re-creations of our own brain systems, like computers. One name for this individual electronic/neurological link-up system could be an 'ibrain'. We have also seen how sometimes the networks that integrate people, or people and things, into a single system can become destructive, for example cycles of abuse or computer addiction. This destructive interconnection has to be broken and the internal brain connections re-established.

Norman Doidge in *The Brain That Changes Itself* tells how cognitive scientist Andy Clark claims we are natural-born cyborgs. "Electronic media are so effective at altering the [brain's] nervous system because both work in similar ways and are basically compatible and thus easily linked. Both involve the instantaneous transmission of electric signals to make linkages. Because our nervous system is plastic [or flexible], it can take advantage of this compatibility and merge with the electronic media, making a single, larger system." Flexible young brains are particularly vulnerable.

Global Brain

In the TV programme *All Watched Over By Machines Of Loving Grace*, humans and machines were described as one global system linked through information. This collective system of individual ibrains could be called a global brain. Derrick de Kerckhove describes this global brain in *The Skin Of Culture*. "The world wide web is growing like the brain of an infant Leviathan. The Internet is the nascent foetus of this collective brain." The concept of a global brain raises two questions: firstly, which part of the human brain has been re-created, and secondly, which kind of thinking then dominates the hybrid system - human or electronic?

To answer question one, we need to look at what the Internet does, and this will gives us a good idea of which part of the brain it reflects. The Internet is able to process vast amounts of information automatically; it reinforces connections between useful pieces of information and its influence is growing. It is not conscious of itself, but the Internet is like a huge uncontrolled market place, where supply meets demand and sometimes leads it, with an underworld just below the surface, the so-called Dark Net.

The part of the brain this most resembles is the autopilot that governs our automatic processes. It too deals with trillions of pieces of information that come in every millisecond from all over the human body network, reinforcing frequently used connections. Like a market, it supplies and anticipates demand, and is at the gateway of our unconscious, primitive urges, behind a web-like structure in the brain.

The autopilot is essential to life, particularly dominant pre-birth and in a child's early years, but needs to be held in check later by more self-aware parts of the brain. Stephen Talbott in *The Future Does Not Compute* talks of computers as a shadow that "consists of all the collective, automatic, sleepwalking, deterministic processes we could yield to." Breaking the connection with automated things will reflect the breaking of the autopilot's increasing role in our lives.

The second question is about whether people use computers as tools, separate from themselves, or is the brain's natural flexibility being misused by adapting to and becoming part of an electronic system? It raises pressing issues about the two-way transmission of information between computer and brain in young people whose brains are very flexible and still developing, and the effect of over-stimulating their unconscious and information-processing centres of the brain. "Could the 'screen experience' be tilting the balance in the brain in favour of the more infantile, senses-driven brain state?" asked Susan Greenfield in *The Times* on 5 November 2011. "Having an exciting, fast-paced interactive experience could increase arousal and in so doing release chemicals which bring about a mindset similar to that of a child, the compulsive eater or even the schizophrenic - a world dominated by raw sensations."

Man or Machine?
Jaron Lanier in *Who Owns The Future* and Evgeny Morozov in *To Save Everything, Click Here* add to the growing concern about the aspiration by some to remake the whole world and its inhabitants "as machine-readable code", to quote Bryan Appleyard in *The Sunday Times* 17 March, 2013. Both books urge us to take back control from the machines, and have a deep distrust of a belief system prevalent in Silicon Valley that puts information-processing above human development.

The question of whether we are creating an 'autistic society' has already been raised, a society of socially underdeveloped, isolated, information geeks, as the automatic processing part of the brain expands more and more, and makes access to more mature parts of the brain difficult - and strengthens the Gut/Primal/Left Side 'rat run'. Susan Greenfield in *The Quest For Identity In The 21st Century* predicts that, "Spending so much time in cyberspace will inevitably lead to brains that are very different from any others in human history".

While Jean Twenge in *The Narcissism Epidemic*, points to a, "Single underlying shift in psychology. America has always been an individualistic nation. (Now there is a) relentless rise of narcissism in our culture. Non-narcissistic people are seduced by the increasing emphasis on material wealth, physical appearance, celebrity worship and attention seeking. The advent of MySpace, Facebook and YouTube may prove to be the second stage in the narcissistic epidemic." A Harvard study has shown that self-disclosure on Facebook delivers powerful chemical rewards to the brain, similar to pleasure from food and sex.

Taking Back Control

Books such as *Rewire Your Brain* by John Arden, *Mindset* by Dr Carole Dweck and Deepak Chopra's *Superbrain* are very useful guides to show how we can change the way our brains work, and help develop its full potential. *The Woman Who Changed Her Brain* by Barbara Arrowsmith-Young is inspiring. The programmes she has developed to help people with specific learning dysfunctions have similarities with the childhood games familiar to older generations. These seem to include activities similar to nursery rhymes and songs, card games, jigsaw puzzles, tracing, telling the time, tongue twisters, fables, playing musical instruments and so on.

These programmes begin simply, are repeated often, and then increase in complexity as each stage is mastered - just as parents have traditionally stimulated their children's brains. Yet the demands of modern life make it difficult for many parents today to have the time to play these games with their children, or perhaps were never taught them themselves. Television is no substitute for the traditional way of learning. What is missing is the emotional energy that passes between people, and even between children and animals, that creates the right environment for learning and change. It is emotional energy that helps the brain put down memories but why use memory when you have Google?

However, the electronic age has transformed human life, by sharing new ideas and triggering revolutionary change, creating a global community regardless of gender, race or age, and by the use of mobile phones in education and 'people power'. There is also a greater understanding that everything is connected. It is also possible that young people particularly have created a new super network in the global brain, using communication to resolve conflict, rather than resorting to aggression, similar to the more typically female brain response to conflict resolution referred to earlier in the book in Chapter 6.

BEYOND THE NET

The global brain that man has created in the Internet is only a limited, partial brain because it does not have emotions or morals, but does it reflect more than the autopilot? The system is going to reflect the brains of those who created it, which means it is masculine and somewhat geeky. Thinking back to Simon Baron-Cohen's thesis of the extreme male brain, it seems that 96% of hackers are male and that those on the autistic spectrum are very comfortable in the cyber world, while having problems with consciousness and face-to-face social interaction. What about the global brain?

Is it Conscious?

Steve Johnson in his book *Emergence* asks, "Will computers become self-aware? Is there a genuine global brain in our future, and will we recognise ourselves in it when it arrives?" Consciousness has puzzled scientists and psychologists for a long time. We saw in Chapter 3 that there are two meanings to the word: one relates to the physical state, and the other sense is psychological, used to describe an awareness of ourselves, others and beyond that grows and develops over time. It is the second meaning we are looking at here. It seems to have links with the ancient belief of the mind's eye or 'third eye', supposedly situated in the middle of the forehead, in the Forebrain.

Rita Carter in *Mapping The Mind* identifies the region of the brain I call the Forebrain as, "The home of consciousness, the high-lit land of self-awareness. It is here mystics have traditionally placed the third eye, the gateway to the highest point of awareness."

The mind's eye is like an inner screen onto which we can project internal information and images, including a picture of ourselves, and which can receive information from other sources. The third eye can be open or closed: when it is closed, we are unaware of things outside our own sensory experience and when it opens, we are conscious or aware of ourselves, others and beyond in a new way. Consciousness, like our thinking, develops in stages over time, helping us connect thoughts and ideas. It can develop slowly, but if we share new ideas with others, we can help 'raise' the level of their consciousness and vice versa.

In the Internet, man too has developed a system over time in the outside world that connects thoughts and ideas, which can be switched on or off and so reflects some of the third eye's abilities. The Internet too has a screen onto which images and information can be projected, with one's pictures on Facebook that are transmitted instantly around the global network. And like the immediate flash of understanding in inspiration that can transform our thinking, so images too can go viral on YouTube or thoughts on Twitter.

The mind's eye is also used by the unconscious when it projects dreams onto its inner screen while we sleep and this seems closer to the computer's role. We have seen that the unconscious can also project internal dramas onto the world outside. An example of the release of the unconscious onto our streets was in the UK riots in London and other cities in 2011 that were fed by violence, revenge and greed, just like the Underground Pit, while mobile phone systems operated under the radar of law and order to evade the security forces, like the criminal underworld.

So the Internet itself is not conscious, but what role does the unconscious play?

Or Unconscious?

So the key question is not whether the Internet is developing its own conscious awareness, but whether the computer screen is being used by the unconscious so that our awareness is going down to its level rather than being raised. Keith Foster in *Lifelight* highlights the degenerative effect of electromagnetic fields to normal biological systems. Normal Doidge points out the effect of Internet pornography on face-to-face relationships. "Softcore pornography's influence is most profound because it influences young people with little sexual experience and especially plastic [flexible] brains, in the process of forming their sexual tastes and desires. Men exposed to porn on the Internet reported increasing difficulty in being turned on by their actual sexual partners".

It is a question of balance between time spent in the virtual world of the man-made screen and time in the real world with real people. It is not a question of Old IT or New IT: either/or thinking is part of the old Left Side thinking. Instead we need to use both Old and New IT as appropriate, with Information Technology playing a supporting not dominant role in our lives, just as the information-processing function of the brain needs to support emotional, psychological and moral development.

Television was the original man-made far-seeing eye, but many of its programmes today now seem to reflect the unconscious world. The Underground Pit operates rather like the criminal underworld, the subject of numerous TV dramas and the many books that now begin with the words 'a body was found...'. On the web too, there is a subterranean Dark Net world of violence, revenge and greed. In *Dark Market*, Misha Glenny points out, "Three fundamental threats face us in the 21st century: cyber crime, cyber warfare and cyber industrial espionage." In cyber crime, people's identities can be stolen and used for criminal purposes. Are parts of our identities being taken down the brain drain, while our brains sometimes confuse the real and virtual screen worlds with catastrophic results?

It is time we opened our real eyes to the fact that young people are in the frontline of a struggle between consciousness and the unconscious, caught up in the web of the individual network I call the ibrain that links brain and electronic devices to an unregulated global brain.

We can however turn things around, and use the brain/electronic link to become more aware of our own inner workings, including the brain's ability to re-create the world in its own image, which at present is being used unconsciously. We need to take that knowledge and use it consciously for the good of all.

BRAIN CHANGE

If man has designed a system that mirrors and reinforces the automatic parts of our thinking, does this make it harder for children to develop the parts of the brain responsible for physical contact, social awareness, emotional maturity and individual responsibility? Susan Greenfield believes that reductions in eye contact, body language, physical actions, and voice - all unavailable on Facebook - are leading to reduced empathy. Empathy, or seeing other people's points of view, is what children need to help them progress as people, and it is also what the world needs in order to respond to the present global crises.

Here we do have to take note of gender differences. Statistically, boys and men have lower empathy scores compared with girls and women; far more boys are autistic than girls; three times as many males have anti-social personality disorder, and three-quarters of narcissists are males. Has this become more of a problem since men stopped learning how to care for others such as animals and younger siblings in a more agrarian society? If so, perhaps re-introducing school farms into education might fill the gap. Carshalton Boys Sports College has shown how this could be done and its beneficial effect on educational standards.

On-screen violence colours one's perception of the world outside, creating a fear of risk, strangers and change which, as was noted earlier, has the same effect on some children as living in a war zone. Crime statistics that contradict this perception are discarded in the face of the repeated visual threats to survival. As we have seen, the needs of children and adults are different: what a mature person can handle safely may be very damaging in the hands of a child, whether that is playing with fire, assessing risk or viewing conflict, but both children and adults now perceive the world as more threatening than before.

Keeping children confined to their homes and projecting danger onto the outside world is not the answer. Integrated Thinking not only integrates inner and outer development, it also rebalances the different parts of the system to create greater harmony, which would then be reflected in our attitude to the outside world.

It is not only children's and adults' brains that can be remoulded: the brain has the potential to change throughout life. We have looked at some of the brain changes in midlife, when unconscious programmes do come to the fore, but only so we can complete unfinished business and lighten the load, before moving on to develop the most evolved part of the brain further, the Forebrain, as part of the process of greater integration.

It may be a surprise to those more used to the focus on youth, but "Dendrites, the branch-like extensions of neurons that facilitate communication between brain cells, reach their greatest density and number from the early fifties to the late seventies", according to Gene Cohen in his book *The Mature Mind*.

The Forebrain is where we have our own internal screen and we need to make greater use of its pattern-identification skills to recognise the similarities between the brain and the machines and networks people create. Then instead of making machines more human-like and people more machine-like, we can use the prism of the global network to understand better how our brains work and what needs to change within.

GAME CHANGE

Sometimes, there is so much to change, so many crises or threats to survival all at once that an existing way of thinking breaks down completely. When that happens, either the unconscious rushes in, or if the collapse is part of the integration process, then older systems are revived that can 'hold the fort' until new connections are made. It is a rather like reverting to snail mail if the Internet crashes, or using a former network of communication such as the direct link between the Monarch and the shires through the Lord Lieutenants if central and local authority should break down.

Collapse or break down, however, can be terrifying, even when it is positive and indicative of change, as when a baby is being born and his world is collapsing around him. In the outside world, it seemed as if the banking system might collapse in 2008, as if law and order had broken down during the 2011 riots in the UK, and the European Union was threatened in 2012 by the economic problems of some of the member states. These could be symptoms of a way of thinking that needs to change, which along with the re-emergence of Primal Brain priorities and activities, are preparing the way for the next stage of development.

We have seen earlier that although there are many ways of thinking, it is men's thinking that has created and come to dominate the social, political and global structures in the world today. We saw earlier that computers and the Internet reflect the male brains who created them, and that it is male brains that created the institutions and businesses we work in, and it is mostly male values that have shaped societies across the world.

We have considered that in creating a society where Left Side of the New Brain's interests in 'things' like money, power and possessions are more important than the Right Side's focus on sharing, caring and comforting people, we are at risk of re-creating the 'extreme male brain', fixated on systems, automation and objects rather than relationships, people and compassion.

153

I have emphasised repeatedly that the core of Integrated Thinking is that it is based on stages of brain development. The development of the Left Side of the New Brain and Western thinking has brought us to the point we are now. If it needs to change, it is not because it - or male-dominated thinking - is wrong. It is because we have reached the next stage of development, when the role of the Left Side of the New Brain becomes supportive rather than dominant, particularly in the West, so that information-processing supports personal and collective growth, when going out to 'bring home the bacon' supports the more important task of bringing up children, and when money, power and possessions are relegated to the world of things not as evidence of a person's worth.

CHAPTER REVIEW

In this chapter, we have seen that, while recognising its benefits, over-dependency on Information Technology, the Old IT, has to change if young people as well as mature adults are to make the best use of their brains. We have also seen how the unconscious has used the Internet to reveal some of its activities on the global stage. We need to appreciate this ability the brain seems to have of being able to re-create itself, and use it consciously so that we can create a more integrated world in the future for everyone.

Integrated Thinking is a mature stage of development, which seeks to bring within an overall framework parts that may be at differing levels of development. It is the same with the world. Some countries have reached a more mature stage of political or economic development, while others are more developed in communal or spiritual areas, but all are essential in the evolving picture of global development. The next chapter will look at some of the problems that could arise during a handover phase from our present way of thinking to a new, more integrated framework.

12 A NEW WORLD ORDER?

This chapter looks at some of the problems that a change from our present way of thinking to a new, more integrated way might cause, including the risk that un-integrated elements from the unconscious could flood in. In addition, one of the main aims of Integrated Thinking is to re-balance the different parts of the whole system in order to follow more closely the pattern of human development, which means that in some cases the order of importance of different parts of the brain is changed.

Also, different nations will respond differently, because they are at differing stages and will need to change in ways that are most appropriate for their particular stage of development, as has happened in communication and economic globalisation.

We also need to look at who might be the most useful guides both externally and internally for this new order, so that this process becomes one of clarity rather than confusion, as the old thinking of right or wrong gives way to a more complex understanding of what is appropriate at this stage of human and global development. This complexity is very much linked to the development of the Forebrain.

To avoid any misunderstanding, I have to emphasise that integration is not a one-off event or a once-and-forever achievement. Even when all the parts have been brought together and integrated, in time one element will begin to move ahead, causing disruption to the other elements so making them change in response, and leading to a new form of greater integration.

WALLS COMING DOWN

Integrated Thinking builds connections between different ways of thinking, and between bodies of knowledge and levels of human activity, but what happens if the Crossing Bridge in the brain is closed, as the crossover point between West and East Berlin could be closed at Checkpoint Charlie?

Instead of a Crossing Bridge, there is a metaphorical wall in many people, like the Berlin wall or the wall on the left bank in Israel. The wall can divide North and South too, seen earlier as separating the Forebrain's ideas and vision from the Primal Brain's application of practical reality. Outside we see how the North/South divide can split the world in two economically, or divide people in the American Civil War or in Korea or Ireland.

Bennett and Sally Shaywitz' experiments at Yale University in 1995 found that men were more likely to have an inner wall than women, for biological and social reasons. Not only are women's brains different from before birth, the Crossing Bridge at the central crossroads of the female brain is bigger and better connected and more likely to stay open. The Crossing Bridge's integrating function has been further strengthened by girls and women taking advantage of Left-Side biased education systems and so balance their natural tendency for Right-Side thinking.

On the other hand, the male tendency to overdevelop their Left Side's ability to separate and put things in compartments means they are more likely to 'wall' off parts of their brain too, that then remain at a less developed level. For some in the West, the Left Side of divisions has become so dominant it is as if the Left Side of the New Brain has divided itself off from the rest of the brain, to become like an island, like Britain. We have seen that if there is no bridge to cross, we have to go down into a tunnel under the wall from an earlier stage of development to rejoin the two Sides of the New Brain. This unconscious journey into a psychological tunnel happens naturally to many in midlife, and is often a disturbing period of change.

Britain has been joined to Europe by a tunnel, but it is at a different stage of development from the EU, and so has not become fully integrated. There is also, as pointed out previously, reluctance in some politicians to lose their hard-won independence. The United Kingdom brought separate countries together politically and economically with a common currency and language centuries ago, while continuing the link between country and crown, Primal and Forebrains. It spread its people, administration and law throughout its empire, yet even after the loss of empire, its culture has spread and its language became global, thanks to the world wide web invented by Britain's Tim Berners-Lee.

The United Kingdom has opened up its borders to immigrants and new ways of doing things, and has opened up its emotional boundaries too, which many date to the response to the death of Princess Diana in 1997.

No longer the country of the stiff upper lip, the opening ceremony of the London 2012 Olympics led the empathy stakes in what Stuart Jeffries in *The Guardian* on 4 August 2012 called, "A festival of emotion, that human connection between spectators and athletes". The release of positive emotions such as empathy can lead to fresh growth on the Tree of Life.

Some see Britain as being on the brink of a new kind of leadership; an article in the *Independent On Sunday* on 19 November 2012 described Britain as now being the most powerful nation on earth, based on Joseph Nye's concept of 'soft power'. "A country may obtain the outcomes it wants in world politics because other countries - admiring its values, emulating its examples, aspiring to its level of prosperity and openness - want to follow it."

If that were true, it would mean the USA renouncing its prime global position in favour of the old country. That would be like expecting the ego to renounce its position in favour of the wisdom of the mature Forebrain, or young people to give up their social dominance to their elders. How likely is that to happen in today's world?

US AND I

Integrated Thinking links personal, political and global development, and aims to increase the use of the Forebrain, including its ability to foresee probable outcomes. If the New IT is found to be a useful guide, then the above outcome in the relative leadership roles of the US and UK might be one of its predictions. It would be in line with what we know about the ego, and especially the Mighty I, which is that in midlife, it has to do the last thing it wants to do and give up control. In a sense, it has to die, to be crossed out and sacrifice itself so that something greater can live. Then there is a form of resurrection as the ego rises again, no longer in control but ready to play its part as supporting role to the True Self.

How far is the UK from this change in the position of the ego and how far is America, the Mighty US? America was created by people who had a strong sense of themselves as individuals, those 'black sheep' who did not fit into what their families or societies expected of them. Freedom of the individual is still very important. Many if not most Americans believe that others follow where the sole superpower leads - and market globalisation enhances that view. George Soros in his book *Open Society* comments that, "The US feels that its superpower status entitles it to dominate international institutions to which it belongs, justified on the grounds of military superiority."

Others see it differently. Michael Lind in his book *Made in Texas* connected, "The traditional Texan businessman with that of the pre-modern 'seigneurial' elite", and that, "At the beginning of 21st century, the USA is experiencing something that happened to Britain, France, Germany and Japan a generation ago in earlier stages of industrial civilisation".

In *The Better Angels Of Our Nature* John Arden, in referring to self-help justice of vigilantism and the law of the gun, states that, "The major regions of USA underwent the civilising process at different times and to different extents. The decline of violence in the American West and South lagged behind the East by two centuries. The one great universal in the study of violence is that most is committed by 15-30 year old men, which was a predominant age group in the American West and South. The Wild West was eventually tamed not just by flinty-eyed marshals, but by an influx of women, who used their bargaining position to transform the West into an environment better suited to their interests". And that environment was better for life generally.

For was it really cowboys who brought people together to make the United States? What about the settlers? We have seen the critical role that women played, but also, as the song says: "The farmer and the cowboy should be friends". Good neighbourliness is what got people through, looking out for each other, caring for the old, the young and the sick - not the lone cowboy, using his weapon to take the law into his own hands.

But still there is reluctance in the US to give up their guns, given the threat to their survival in the War on Terror. The attack on the heart of world trade on 11 September 2001 was like a midlife heart attack, coming out of the blue, when survival itself is threatened. The US did survive, but did it change its way of thinking or did it initially continue to play the global cowboy? Susan Faludi in *The Terror Dream* saw 9/11 as presenting an opportunity to show America's character as a society, but that the actual response seemed to have little bearing on the circumstances, but instead was based on the American masculine archetype from the 19th century frontier, of Man the Hunter in his role as cowboy.

However change is in the air. We saw earlier how someone who has had experience of different cultures finds change easier. They also are less likely to suffer from deliberate blindness to the faults and failings of a system. We have also seen how women, particularly after midlife, can have greater inner integration, and when in positions of power they have the potential to change the world again, "Into an environment that better suits their interests" - to repeat the earlier quote from John Arden.

SPRING AND AUTUMN

The most turbulent times in families can be when parents are having their own midlife crisis in the autumn of their lives at the same time that their children reach their spring-time adolescence. We have seen that there are similarities between the two stages, a similarity that Barbara Tuchman in *A Distant Mirror* saw reflected in Europe's own 14th century adolescence and the 20th century more mature development, for what happens in individual families can also occur collectively, in different areas of the globe. One example when this familial turbulence was replicated in the outside world was during the Arab Spring and the European Autumn of 2011, the first being a call for greater democracy and power-sharing and the second when economic stability was threatened in the European Union.

Democracy, you will remember, is related to the New Brain stage of development, and the growth of justified anger, respect, regret and empathy on the Tree of Life. The call for democracy arises when those who have been led by a dominant authority figure demand their freedom to choose their lives for themselves, like children rejecting the authoritarian patriarch in a traditional family.

Most Western societies have already had their 'teenage' rebellions, in past civil wars, revolutions and republics. Adolescents are idealistic, challenge authority, and create a mess. In the past 20 years, it has been terrorists from developing countries who challenged the authority of the West, creating a holy mess, fired up by an uncompromising idealism, at the same time that the West was facing its own crisis.

Now, however, the focus of the revolutionaries is closer to home, to their own restrictive regimes, rather than blaming a distant 'them'. In the West, we can help them make that crossing safely over the bridge from authoritarianism to democracy, by ensuring individual freedom also comes with responsibility for others, so that leaders do not fall back into tribal allegiances and the pursuit of money, power and possessions - but only if we lead by example. Like a parent, we can give guidelines and support, intervene if absolutely necessary, but we cannot determine the outcome; that would be like trying to make our children into replicas of ourselves.

The structures and systems necessary for democracy to develop have to be reflected in the internal development of the people responsible for their administration. Paddy Ashdown in *Swords And Ploughshares* identifies the need for people, "Equally at home in all government departments, rather than developing politicians or diplomats or soldiers or aid workers". That very much fits in with the New IT.

However, integration may not be the most appropriate stage in all situations. The different parts have to be at a similar stage of development before they can be integrated. The Eurozone ignored economic differences between nations to promote consensus on the single currency, yet not all countries were at the same monetary stage. Some nations were more fiscally responsible, while the systems and structures of others were at an earlier stage of development, with a few still turning a blind eye to corruption.

A television programme on *The Great Euro Crash* expressed the view that money cannot hold disparate parts together; political committed will must come first. Sometimes structures have to reach breaking point, even collapse as in physical illness or fall apart in crises or catastrophes, to be restructured in a new, stronger way.

EMERGENCE

If our present leaders are ones who have succeeded in the present way of thinking, it may be difficult for them to let go a mental construct that has stood them in such good stead. So we need to look at who or what could guide us as the New IT emerges. What is emerging from this exploration of the world through the prism of Integrated Thinking is that there are similarities between the stage of life we know as a midlife crisis and the present stage of global development.

Those who have been through a midlife crisis in their own lives know the changes and adaptations that have to be made, and most importantly, they know they emerge the other side, changed but with renewed confidence for the challenges ahead. Some changes in midlife are physical: the need to reconsider ways of eating and living, perhaps having to downsize, conserve energy, keep active and even revalue old skills. There are emotional changes too: sometimes anger that things have not turned out the way they planned, there is the fear of an uncertain future, the loss of ego control as things long 'held on ice' in the unconscious flood out threatening emotional stability, but also a greater compassion for others. Then there are the mental changes: letting go long held mental constructs, changes to our internal and external image, no longer striving to be 'sexy'. And there are economic changes too, making do with less, philanthropic giving rather than acquiring, as the drive for money, power and possessions decreases.

How do these changes relate to the present global crises? Could the earth be having its own midlife crisis? Al Gore thinks so. "Is our species now on the verge of a kind of midlife crisis?" he asks in *Earth In The Balance*.

Scientists tell us we are past our peak in energy terms. Politicians tell us we have to make do with less. Doctors tell us we have to eat less. Surveys show that people are concerned for the future. Environmentalists warn of ice melting. Yes, the media still seems to act as if everyone should be 'sexy' and older women are not considered suitable as TV presenters (clinging onto youth is a familiar sign of a midlife crisis!) but even here there are signs of change.

Recent personal and global changes could be described as emergencies or as something new emerging, for these changes are critical to rebalancing the different parts of the brain, and in particular, making best use of the rewired Forebrain, the centre of wisdom. Older people can make use of the Forebrain's hindsight, seeing the consequences of past actions and wanting to put mistakes right; and also insight, that greater awareness of ourselves and others, as well as overseeing and taking the long view. At the same time there is an often-unexpected awareness of time speeding up, urgency rather than emergency.

An additional attribute of maturity is that one's perspective or consciousness of the circle around one increases, from the family circle to the wider community and then to the global family, understanding humanity's connectivity which leads to a concern for the future of all. It is this connectivity, concern and expanding circles that will help guide us in the future.

SECTION REVIEW

In chapters 9 and 10 of this Section, we have looked at history, global crises and conflicts; in chapter 11 we reflected on the limits of Information Technology, the old IT, and its effect on the brain and development, and in the final chapter of the Section, we considered if a new world order could be emerging from this period of change.

Using the framework of brain development that has already been applied to social and political development, we can see parallels in the world outside with the key stage of change called the midlife crisis. This could form the basis of a new approach to global politics, and for a new kind of leadership less youth- or competition-orientated.

A key question for this Section to address was who needs to change? The answer is we all do, but in different ways appropriate to our own time and place. If we take what we know about human development and use it as a framework for other kinds of developments, then social, political and global changes become more familiar, more positive and more integrated.

I have mostly used these similarities between the different developments as an analogy; some may think the similarities are co-incidental, but there is also the possibility that they indicate something more exciting - the power to create the world in our own image. I have put forward the proposal that the brain seems to use itself as a model for the systems and structures it creates in the outside world. This has been largely unconscious, but if we were to use this process consciously, what kind of world would we be able to create?

Before we take that step, however, we need to look at what is missing from this new framework. There is another source of knowledge that has to be integrated, the world of the Mind and spirit, which is the subject of the final Section of the book, Section 4.

SECTION 4

SPIRITUAL DEVELOPMENT

"The more deeply I search for the roots of the global environmental crisis, the more I am convinced that it is an outer manifestation of an inner crisis, that is - for want of a better word - spiritual"
Al Gore

INTRODUCTION

In previous Sections, we have looked at our present ways of thinking and why they need to change; in this Section we will consider what might be still missing from the bigger picture by reviewing the belief constructs the brain has developed since the beginning of human life on earth. The earth is one part of a much bigger system and subject to forces from outside the earth that we cannot see: it is the same with the brain. This Section looks at the forces we cannot see which affect our brains, sometimes called the world of the Mind and spirit. Both need to be integrated into the new framework if the New IT is to be true to its name.

Chapter 13 integrates spiritual development into the personal, political and global model. Mind and spirit are difficult concepts to pin down: I will give my own definition of 'Mind' in Chapter 14, and use the word 'spiritual' in the sense of the awareness of something beyond ourselves, above the Tree of Life. 'Religion' refers to the branch of knowledge that different peoples have devised to codify this awareness in a way appropriate for their time and stage of development.

Integration embraces disintegration as part of the whole process, for example the disintegration of unwanted or incorrect brain connections or networks involved in brain pruning. In Chapter 15, however, we also need to look at what happens when the unconscious forces of disintegration and destruction are not just twisted but cut off from the integrating process and go it alone, like troops under Marlon Brando in the film *Apocalypse Now*. Even more destruction is caused when these forces re-enter human thinking and behaviour through gaps in our mental constructs, yet remain 'outside the command structure'. I believe this negative force is what we call evil, and disarming it is essential if the integrating process is not to stall or be sabotaged.

The final chapter in the book reviews what might be missing from our present understanding and belief constructs to finish this introduction to Integrated Thinking. We have had religions that worship the Mother, then God The Father and The Son - who is needed to complete the family line-up?

13 TRUST

The awareness that there is something else to life beyond what people can see is the basis of religion and this awareness is associated with the Forebrain's third eye of consciousness and conscience. If we want to develop more of our Forebrain's capabilities, we need to include the wisdom of the ages and sages.

Since earliest times, religions have tried to explain the unseen forces operating on people from above and below, and to reveal patterns of human development yet to come in ways that were time and place appropriate. Trust or belief is using a particular explanation or overall mental construct as the basis for how one lives one's life. We all have belief systems we trust in, even free marketeers who believe in the 'invisible hand' of capitalism, although they perhaps would not think of that as their religion.

Modern man may dismiss former mental constructs as unscientific but there is much that is outside the scientific model that can have profound effects on our lives. It is possible that ancient peoples, often after undergoing long periods of discipline and training, had access to knowledge that can be hidden from those who are on the ladder of success or from those who need tangible evidence, such as scientists, sceptics or those with autism.

Today it is easier to visualise how knowledge can be stored outside our brains yet accessible to them, now that we can use the analogy of cyberspace and clouds - yet the Internet is vulnerable to underground sabotage, and so too is this higher level of consciousness.

I want to emphasise again that integration does not mean that different dimensions of development are identical. The differences between personal psychology and spiritual development are explained well in Susan Howatch's '*Starbridge*' novels.

One example of what happens when the personal and spiritual are confused will highlight the problem. When a child realises that his parents engage in sexual activity, he protects himself from the overwhelming feeling of being excluded by telling himself that they only do 'it' to have babies. If this immature psychological defence, that sex is for procreation only, becomes a dogma of faith, it can cause millions of unwanted pregnancies when contraception is forbidden, and affect attitudes towards homosexual partnerships. To say nothing of a priest's immature sexual development finding an outlet in sex with children.

As with other Sections of the book, the key to spiritual development is the more evolved use of the Forebrain, including directing primitive drives towards more enlightened or more productive goals.

RELIGIONS

I can only speak from my own background of Christianity, which is based on the knowledge that one man shared of his spiritual understanding with people 2,000 years ago as recorded in the New Testament and elsewhere. The question often asked is whether the Bible is historically accurate or scientifically provable. No, but neither are our memories historically accurate yet they guide us throughout our lives.

And how do you prove love scientifically? That would be impossible, yet we all know it exists and the effect it can have on us. My view of the Bible is that through the account of one tribe, the Jews and the breakaway group of early Christians, it tells the story of the journey we are all engaged in, from instinctive unconscious beings to conscious awareness. It is a story that is continuing today, in which neuroscience is now playing an important role.

Repeating Pattern

For those who find this area of life unfamiliar or uncomfortable, I am going to look at spiritual development through the model for intellectual development that forms the framework for Integrated Thinking. You will recall that in Section 2, we saw how a baby's world at the Primal Brain stage centres on his mother as an all-powerful protector, as he instinctively explores the world around him. With the development of the Right Side of the New Brain, he learns the rules from his family, traditionally led by a dominant father, and this process continues in his early school days.

Later as an adolescent, education teaches him principles that have to be applied differently in different situations, giving him a degree of self-responsibility and developing the analytical skills and the Left Side of the New Brain. Then at University, particularly at MA or PhD level, the student is mature enough for self-direction, something that would have caused chaos at earlier stages.

Each stage reflects the development of the four main parts of the brain, and each incorporates or builds on earlier stages, which is how the brain itself develops. The stages are universal and inbuilt, but people in whom this process is accelerated in religion are called mystics or prophets.

If we apply this basic pattern to spiritual development, we see that the first 'instinctive' religions were based on Mother, just as a baby's world is centred on her: there was Mother Nature, Mother Earth and the pagan goddesses. This honouring of the mother was reflected in art, culture and matriarchal societies.

The next stage was when the Jewish 'family' or tribe received written rules handed down from God the Father to his chosen people. Jonah Lehrer in *The Decisive Moment* speaks of how, "Moral emotions existed long before Moses. Religion allows us to codify these intuitions. The details of the 10 commandments reflect the details of the evolved moral brain". Instead of many gods, there was just one single identity known as Jehovah or I AM.

I Am

This corresponds to the Right Side of the New Brain pattern of learning the family/tribe rules, with a dominant father as sole authority. In Judaism the mother religions were banned. Each new stage is meant to incorporate key elements from the previous stage, not reject them. Is it possible that the Jews sublimated the yearning for a lost 'mother' into their all-encompassing desire for a return to their lost motherland? For Jewish men, circumcision compounded the earlier cutting of the umbilical cord that separated mother and baby.

In Chapter 3 I referred to the internal stage of development when the unique person emerges from the potential stock characters in the unconscious by repressing certain elements, and how this is similar to the stage when the belief in gods and goddesses was superseded by the belief in One God.

However, in the reshaping of gods and goddesses with positive and negative attributes into the belief construct of one male, all good God, the feminine and negative aspects were excluded. For some the feminine and the negative were linked and projected onto women themselves.

Jesus Christ brought the concept of individual identity down to the personal level, not just something reserved for the God of the Jews. "Jesus speaks of the innermost I AM, the essential identity of every man and woman," says Eckhart Tolle in *A New Earth*. Jesus opened up the way for everyone to cross the bridge from tribal allegiance to the 'I am' or ego of individuality, moving on from rules to principles but not overturning them. Jesus' principle of "Love your neighbour as yourself" still resonates today, as we try to balance our individual and collective needs, and the Two Sides of the New Brain. Some Jews followed the new way but for others, the Father and the collective, tribal level was too powerful. However, when that vital crossing is denied and individual initiative discouraged, seeing oneself as a victim can explain away a lack of self-responsibility. This can also be true collectively of a nation.

Diversion

Here I am making a small diversion on the spiritual journey to show its relevance to the world today. Karen Armstrong in *Battle for God* points out that many fundamentalist religions neglect the compassionate teachings of their founders in favour of theologies of rage, resentment and revenge, recalling the earliest depiction of God in the Old Testament - and the Underground Pit of twisted emotion. Deepak Chopra in *How To Know God* also links the God of the Old Testament with the Old Brain and the unconscious.

In the case of the Jewish people, although they saw themselves initially as the 'chosen people', linking God with the settlement stage of human development, over time they became a scapegoat for social ills and associated with money - similar to the role of the unconscious.

When the Jews finally were returned to the Promised Land after World War II as reparation for their suffering, they regurgitated their repressed anger onto others, which is how an overloaded Underground Pit too spills out its contents. In returning home, they also re-enacted a story told long ago of the conflict between two children of the same father.

In Jesus' story of the Prodigal Son, the one son took his special inheritance as a right, not as a responsibility. He wasted it, wandering far and wide. He suffered greatly, but finally returned home, helped by the open arms of the father. He was given back his old place, but the other son had a grievance. He'd lost out, been displaced; there was no rejoicing for him. He felt no one understood, and no one listened. There the story ended, 2,000 years ago, without a resolution of the conflict. In history, two nations, one Jewish and the other Arab, are both children of the same heavenly Father. After wandering far and wide and suffering greatly, the Jewish people returned home in 1948, helped by an open arms deal. They have been given their own place back - but what about the Arabs and their grievance? They have lost out, been displaced, but no one listened to them.

How will the story end today?

Christianity

Returning to the main Jewish/Christian story, Jonathan Sachs in his book *The Great Partnership* explores the link between brain development and the Judaic/Christian tradition just as Iain McGilchrist linked brain development and Western history (see Chapter 9). The New Testament was written in Greek, a language which Jonathan Sachs describes as, "The unmistakable signature of the [Left Side]. Greece and Israel in antiquity offer us the sharpest possible contrast between a strongly left-side and a strongly right-side culture. Western civilisation was born in the synthesis between Athens and Jerusalem brought about by Pauline Christianity and the conversion of Emperor Constantine ....that led to the intellectual edifice of Western civilisation until 17th century".

Typically Left Side however, was the way the West assimilated knowledge from the East without giving it credit. "Historically, Islamic scholars in the fields of philosophy, medicine, mathematics, chemistry and astrology helped sow the seeds of the Enlightenment in Europe", wrote Said Ghazali in *The Independent*, 15 September 2012.

The Christian Church did not universally welcome the path to individuality. Richard Tarnas in *Passion Of The Western Mind* notes that, "The assertion of human individuality in early Christianity was largely negated in favour of the submission of the individual to the Church's moral, intellectual and spiritual authority". The all-powerful Father was too strong, and Jesus' integration of justice with the other side of the Tree of Life, mercy, was lost as the Left Side justified the power of the Church hierarchy.

Jonathan Sachs again: "From the 17th century onwards, first science, then philosophy declared their independence from theology and the great arch stretching from Jerusalem to Athens began to crumble". And so the bridge between the two Sides of the New Brain also began to crumble, increasing the separation and development of the Left Side of the New Brain in the West.

Differences

For Jonathan Sachs, "Dualism (the splitting of good and bad) resolves the internal conflict of cognitive dissonance by saying that 'it wasn't us, it wasn't God, so it must be Them'". So internal conflict was and is projected onto 'others' outside in the name of religion, each branch convinced only they have the 'truth', rather than recognising that as with stages of personal development, there are stages in spiritual development that are time and place appropriate.

It is not only Muslims who react to challenges to their faith. When a Paris cinema showed a film in the 90's in which Christ appeared to make love to Mary Magdalene, the cinema was burnt down and one person was killed. As with all kinds of development, Integrated Thinking seeks to integrate the different stages of spiritual development and recognise that all have their value, including the final stage of spiritual inner self-direction without the need for a male-dominated hierarchical structure. This is the stage many in the West are entering now, trying to integrate information from other religions, in a similar way that knowledge from the West and East in medicine, technology and psychology is also being integrated.

It is not that one kind of understanding is better than another; we need all the different understandings to form the whole picture, just as we need all the different parts of the brain. Do you remember the story of the elephant and the blindfolded men in Chapter 1, and how by focusing on one part only, we miss out on the whole? We have much to learn from each other, yet it is difficult to let go long held belief systems, those inner mental constructs or temples that hold our most treasured beliefs, particularly when life is uncertain.

Other people who are more used to clearly defined concepts that can be scientifically replicated or proven, find religious belief constructs hard to grasp because the ideas and language are unfamiliar, fuzzy or ill-defined, or because their conscious development has not progressed to awareness of others and/or beyond.

IMAGES AND WORDS

This response by those more familiar with the scientific or analytical model is not surprising, because the unseen spiritual world is difficult to get to grips with, the ideas and language can seem fuzzy, hard to understand and easy to dismiss, but it is in grappling with these issues that the Forebrain and higher consciousness are stimulated. Images such as diagrams, symbols, visual aids or even acting out are particularly helpful in this situation as they can speak to all people, regardless of time or place, and they can reach parts of the human system such as the unconscious and the imagination that applications such as logic just don't reach.

Imagery

Think back to the Berlin Wall: that was a very strong symbol of the wall dividing capitalism and communism, and although that particular wall has come down in the world outside, a mirror image still stands inside many people, so that anything that smacks of 'socialism' in America is rejected. In the eighties, when the Berlin Wall fell, the image that still stood strong in America, the home of the free, was that of the cowboy, the lone gunman, the one who wins, updated to the loner on the stock market in the modern world, his braces replacing a holster, but with an equally quick finger on the trigger, making a killing, re-enacting the role of Man the Hunter for the modern age.

Why did acting out that image continue to dominate instead of changing to Man the Shepherd after man became a farmer? Yet Man the Shepherd is an image that can be resurrected and given new life today, especially if you add it to the image or symbol of the cross at the crossroads of the brain, the Wounded Body. Carl Jung believed that the image of a cross and circle had particular resonance in our brains at midlife as the symbol of integration and the True Self. And Man the Shepherd fits in with the choice to change from competition to caring for others that many men make in midlife, and is increasingly made by younger men too.

Compassion, empathy and mercy from the emotional development of the Tree of Life are central to this care for others and to our spiritual development. "Feelings form the basis for what humans have described for millennia as the human soul", says Antonio Damasio in *Descartes' Error*. Mercy balances out justice and includes forgiveness, which is more than accepting an apology. To for-give means turning something negative into something positive, to GIVE good FOR bad rather than the old way which was to return bad with bad, anger with anger, violence with violence. Steven Pinker refers to the latter kind of retaliation as violent self-help by which people secured justice before that role was handed to the state by law and the will of the people.

Power of the Word

As important as they are, images can only take us so far. Words truly are magic, they open up new worlds and marked a huge leap forward in human development. Words bring light into the darkness of the unconscious, as they take what was unknown and give it a name, embodying ideas or thoughts so that they become real, and become a 'thing' the Left Side of the New Brain can examine, analyse, play with and use, rather than neglect or reject.

Words, like music, also have the power to move us, and release blocks in the Emotional Wheel. As with any skill, once we become proficient at speaking and it becomes automatic, it is so easy to forget what a miracle language is. Written language was even more special: thoughts, ideas and memories could be shared with all people for all time. It was very precious, seen as a gift from God, and so was originally kept for the chosen few, in a similar way that Bibles were kept only for priests until the Reformation.

I wonder how many of you recognise this symbol from the time before the computer: \ ? It is the shorthand symbol for 'p' or 'b'. Shorthand is usually written without vowels, so \ can mean pay or ape, buy or bough - and so on - depending on its thickness and position on a line.

Early Jewish script also was written without vowels. Only the chosen few, the priests, had the secret code of five vowels to unlock the mystery of the word of God: IEOUA, more easily pronounced as JEHOVAH. This was the name of God, the letter of the Law. But the Law has to be lived in the spirit as well as to the letter, so if, according to early Christian beliefs, you add the Jewish symbol for fire or passion, SH, to God's name, you bring the word alive. It becomes IEOSHUA or JESUS, a variant of Joshua.

What's in a Name?

Using the name of Jesus in prayer creates a protected link for knowledge to flow between the brain and above and to protect from an unwanted inflow from the unconscious. The nearest equivalent I can think of is a password to an Internet account that protects from identity fraud and viruses, while allowing access to wider knowledge.

The name of Jesus, however, does more than protect and give access to knowledge; it also confers power and authority. The English legal system is a pale reflection of the Law that governs the unseen worlds of the Mind and spirit, but three legal powers that can be given by and to individuals under English law may help clarify the power of Jesus' name:

1. *Power of attorney.* During your lifetime, you can give this power to someone you trust to have access to all your resources. They stand in your place, and act only in your best interests. This is the power given to Jesus when a person becomes a Christian. He stands in the place of one's egotistical self to act in one's best interests.

2. *Power of arrest.* Jesus' name gives Christians the authority to act in the spiritual underworld in the name of the Law. When squatters take over a building, only police can remove them in the name of the law. It is the same with demons, those internal illegal squatters or bits of discarded personality, that have taken up residence in the Underground Pit. The power of Jesus' name will remove them to a place of security and justice.

176

3. *Power of executor.* When someone dies, an executor carries out the deceased's wishes as contained in his last will and testament. After Jesus' death on the cross, Christians were given the power to carry out his testimony and to bring 'heaven on earth' (see chapter 14). Every time Christians pray in Jesus' name, they call down spiritual power from above to carry out this work on earth.

If people misuse legal powers, they are accountable as trustees. It is the same with spiritual powers. Prayers and these powers create a bottom-up and top-down safe link between domains. It seems as if, without a request for help for oneself or on behalf of others, God - in whatever mental construct that word is used - can only intervene directly in very exceptional circumstances, like a doctor or psychiatrist.

SERVICE

We will look more closely at evil as a force for disintegration separate from the integrating process in Chapter 15, but here we are looking at it within the context of religion. Just as there is a struggle between the unconscious and the conscious, so there is a struggle in the spiritual world between dark and light, between evil and good. Both require sacrifice and hard work to reconcile within the overall picture.

Using war, aggression and the army as imagery for the struggle against the spiritual forces of evil has disadvantages. It encourages the idea of anger being met with anger. Also war is no longer a personal experience for many in the West today.

However, if we change the analogy from an army to a police service, then it brings it closer to home. For like the effects of crime, the effects of evil can be felt even if the perpetrators are unseen. It also brings in the idea of service, duty of care, trust, protection, the law and justice. As we saw in the previous paragraphs, it also fits in with the powers conferred by the name of Jesus, of bringing something from the dark into the light, from the hidden underworld into the scrutiny of the law.

The entry points to the criminal and spiritual underworlds are very similar. Any crack in a person that can be opened up to their advantage will be used to siphon off energy or willpower, in a similar way that criminals siphon off money and goods through gaps in our personal or collective security. It is an undercover world which offers its own mafia-type protection, "Do as I say, or else", while threatening reprisals to those who break its code of silence to tell the truth, rather like the gutter press seems recently to have held the threat of exposure and negative publicity over those in the public eye. It is a spiritual underworld that has hacked its way into our world.

Today, the traditional vices of the spiritual underworld, such as gluttony, lust, greed, vanity and pride, are still with us. We all have them. The difference, according to Christopher Jamison in *Finding Happiness* is, "Between those who have noticed that these thoughts need to be wrestled with, and those who have not". I would argue that far from being wrestled with, it would seem as if the narcissistic tendencies in society today would see these vices as qualities to be celebrated.

Christopher Jamison also talks about the vice of spiritual apathy as appearing to, "Bear some similarity to what modern psychoanalysis calls a midlife crisis". The doctrine of the Trinity could also be linked to modern psychoanalysis: the superego authority of the Father, the individualistic ego of the Son, the ego-ideal or perfect partner of the Holy Spirit, with the devil as our primitive id.

The stronger the links between different domains, rather than specialised compartments with their own exclusive language, the more integrated the branches of human knowledge become, and the stronger the link between the two functions of the brain will be.

We also increase our empathy by focussing on what we have in common rather than focussing on differences, which can lead to the Left Side either/or thinking of good or bad, right or wrong.

SACRIFICE

We can also view the pattern of growth in the Christian Church itself through the mirror of the brain's pattern of development. In its early days, the Church struggled to survive; then it became part of a bigger family, the Roman connection, like the transition from Primal Brain to the Right Side of the New Brain. As it developed, the Church formed part of the linear thinking of institutional order that underpins Left Side Western development, with alternative, more diverse ways of knowing banned, and women airbrushed out of the picture. Then came the increasing power of the Mighty I, the ego of Henry VIII, who broke with the Holy Father to become Head of Church and State. There is a continuing fascination with this period in history, somewhat similar to the fascination with our own adolescent times.

Some Christians preferred to stay with the Catholic Church, with its emphasis on obeying the Father, the importance of ritual and the group rather than individual independence and enquiry. In both branches, women continued to be subservient. And what of the Church's role today? Christianity appears in some places to be growing in countries where self-determination is also growing, as if it was a spiritual companion to democracy - while in the West, Christianity is at its own crossroads. The Church calls itself the body of Christ, yet Christ allowed his body to be broken so that the Spirit could live. Is the Church, as Christ's body, willing to follow Jesus' example by crossing out its own self-justifying ego, and sacrifice itself as the body of Christ so that the Holy Spirit can live?

Earlier we spoke of Christians being like a police service rather than an army. Today it seems to some that the Church is like a police force that concentrates on petty crimes, and on the sexual dimension of the passion spectrum rather than the spiritual, leaving the far more dangerous activities of evil or organised spiritual crimes to flourish in the underworld. But if the Church does not speak out about this area of the spiritual world, who will?

CHAPTER REVIEW

In this chapter, we have considered the similarity between the pattern of human brain development and the growth in religious understanding. In order to 'deconstruct' some of the mysteries, I have tried to show what lies behind the use of certain images and words, and considered the history and potential next step for the Christian Church. I hope this brief review makes spiritual development more accessible and shows its links to other branches of knowledge and to the world today.

Now we turn to the world of the Mind to see where it fits into brain development and Integrated Thinking.

14 MIND

In this chapter, we are entering the world of the Mind, which scientists are only now beginning to explore. However, it is not a completely unknown domain as its workings were known in earlier times under different names, for example, by describing the worlds of the brain and the Mind as the kingdoms of earth and heaven. The ancients did not have our technological inventions; when they wanted to understand themselves and the world, they used their Minds. "As within, so without" and "Know yourself" are phrases dating back thousands of years, but it is only today that we are beginning to realise the depth of these understandings.

John Arden in *Rewire Your Brain* refers to several ways in which access to the Mind can be achieved, by slowing the brainwaves through mindfulness, prayer or open focus. He tells how mindfulness practice cultivates positive feelings, promotes calm and increases attention skills and helps rewire the brain.

We have been looking at how the social, political, global and spiritual worlds reflect the workings of brain development, but is the brain itself a reflection of the Mind? Deepak Chopra in *Superbrain*, claims, "The brain is only the physical representation of the Mind. The real creator is Mind". Paul Hawker in *Soul Survivor* quotes James Jeans as saying, "It may be that each individual consciousness is a brain cell in a universal Mind". Earlier I have used phrases such as 'the brain *seems* to use itself as a template'. This is because I think it is more likely that it is the Mind that is doing this work, rather than the brain.

TO BOLDY GO

There is no scientific agreement about what is the difference between brain and Mind, nor agreement on how they work together. The brain and the Mind seem to be like sex and love: they can be linked, separate or confused with each other. Jeffrey Schwartz offers one description of their relationship in *The Mind And The Brain*: "The brain is the physical embodiment of the Mind, the organ through which the Mind finds expression and through which it acts in the world." Scientists or surgeons cannot examine or see the Mind physically, unlike the brain during surgery, in brain scans or after death. "While theoretically it might be possible for neuroscientists to know everything there is to know about the physical structures and activities of the brain, the Mind, with its thoughts, ideas, impressions and emotions, would still remain unaccounted for", is James Le Fanu's view in his book *Why Us?*

What some scientists call the Mind, I call 'mental constructs', those internal virtual structures we build with the brain's connections to house our memory, consciousness and representations of people, things and ourselves. I reserve the word 'Mind' for something specific although I recognise my straightforward definition may be too simplistic for some working in this complex field. For me, the fundamental difference between the brain and the Mind is that the brain is human, the Mind is superhuman; the brain is limited by time and space, the Mind is not. They are connected through the Forebrain's mind's eye in the forehead, but can operate independently.

My image of the Mind is as our minder, the Hidden Watcher who watches out for us and observes what we do. This presence is also called the Atman, the True Self of psychology, Universal Love or the Christ within. Unlike the brain and the body, the Mind does not die. Deepak Chopra asserts that, "The world's traditions declare that death cannot touch the True Self". Carl Jung saw the Self as an inner guide, the totality of human potential.

182

The Mind's first role is to serve mankind and we can access our Mind through the mind's eye, like accessing the Internet and cyberspace through our computer screen. The reverse happens to us all when we sleep. This is when the Mind uses its link with the unconscious to leave messages or images on our inner screen. Who hasn't gone to sleep with a question, problem or memory failure and woken up with the answer? Our Mind is our very own Google at work while we rest, and a transfer of information can also happen to some people while they are awake, in mystical experiences. The Mind operates on much longer wavelengths than our brains, so linking up is easier when we are relaxed, as in prayer, meditation or just relaxing. Think of all those 'inspirations' in bed, in the bath or under an apple tree.

Yet the Mind can play a much bigger role in our lives than merely answering questions. With the Mind as the brain's master, not its servant, to quote from the ever-popular TV programme *Star Trek*, we can all, "Boldly go where no man has gone before". Or woman. "Understanding how the faculties of the Mind work is a frontier of modern science", is Jeffrey Schwartz' view. Or as Jane and Grant Solomon write in *Harry Oldfield's Invisible Universe*, "The Mind has no boundaries. In our Mind we have the vehicle with which we can be truly universal explorers".

The 'Starship Enterprise' is a modern image for the Mind, travelling at the speed of light, its crew symbolising the Mind's superhuman powers (also called charismatic gifts). We are drawn to those with these powers, like a tractor beam dragged ships towards the Enterprise, and a few can see the charismatic aura that attracts others to its orbit.

In place of the Primal Brain's role of taking care of our bodies, there is the Mind's power of miraculous healing; in place of the Right Side of the New Brain's communication skills is the Mind's communication link across time and space which we can tap into in prayer; and then there is the logic and information skills of the Left Side transformed into superhuman knowledge.

These powers were played out in the TV programme through the characters of 'Bones' the doctor, Uhura and Dr Spock, with the Captain on the bridge. There is even an invisible God-like Mission Control in charge. The Starship Enterprise's original role was to bring back souls lost on previous missions, like the search for those neglected and missing parts of ourselves we all need to undertake if we are to be fully integrated as people.

The Mind has the master, uncorrupted programme of human development that we can download to bring these missing parts back into wholeness or holiness by rewiring our faulty brain connections and creating new networks. One way is the bottom-up, hard path of devoted discipline, which can take a lifetime; the other is top-down, sometimes called 'grace' but both can change the way we think, feel, behave and believe. The Mind can also help remove blocks in our understanding, protect us and get us back on track safely, yet it can only transform its role from servant to master once the ego willingly lets go control.

MESSAGE

Earlier we saw how the ego or 'I' of independence and individuality developed to meet the challenges of adulthood, but midlife is a time when the ego has to let go control and leave the stage, to return in a new form. The paradox is that the ego can only let go control if is strong, detached and has first taken the hard path away from family and group loyalty into personal responsibility. This is not a new idea.

Role Model

Two thousand years ago the man we know as Jesus Christ revealed the Forebrain stage of emotional development in the greater understanding of God as a loving father who balances justice with mercy, not the old God of revenge and retribution from the Primal Brain's Underground Pit. He also revealed the next stage of progress by offering himself as a role model for the development and death of the ego.

He brought the concept of I AM down to earth, the development of the ego's individual identity, no longer an attribute of God alone. He began by moving from group dependency of family ties and tribal loyalties to individual responsibility, from 'us' to 'I', and into a one-to-one personal relationship with God - but that was not the end of the story.

Having developed a strong sense of independent identity, he showed that the next step was to sacrifice the ego or 'I', to cross it out literally and symbolically, and to submit, to suffer, to serve and obey, rather than control, lead, dominate or order. He chose Jerusalem, the crossroads of the ancient world, where this next stage of human development was played out. Just as Christ came back to life in a new form, sometimes unrecognisable, so the ego, having 'died', can rise again in a new form to play a supporting role to the True Self.

Ego and True Self are modern terms devised by psychology to describe different elements within the whole person; in previous times they might have been described as the Son of Man and the Son of God, as a way of differentiating these two stages of human development. Similarly, both the *corpus callosum* or Wounded Body at the brain's crossroads and the wounded body on the cross in Christianity both try to integrate or reconcile differences and conflicts caused by cognitive dissonance or 'sin', when we act in ways that do not reflect our True Self.

Realising that the long-established and arduous bottom-up way of accessing the Mind was not for everyone, nor the discipline and training required to make sure the Mind's powers were not taken over by the ego, Jesus revealed the top-down way to access the Mind safely that could be followed by individuals who could continue to live in the world outside by following his model. He also revealed the powers of the Mind through miracles.

Jesus used stories, actions and symbolic imagery to share this new understanding, as today's knowledge of brain and human stage development was not then available.

Before widespread literacy, imagery and symbolism were more important 2,000 years ago as a way of passing on knowledge to later generations that could be understood by all. Christianity however, like many other religions, split after the death of its founder, perhaps reflecting the different routes the knowledge followed, through authoritative instruction via the Left Side, or through emotional intuition and the Right Side of the New Brain.

In Christianity, it was the Left Side that triumphed through its association with the linear-thinking, male-dominated Roman Empire, yet in recent years there has been a resurgence of interest in the role of the hidden, intuitive knowledge and in women, perhaps realising that something is missing from the Christian story.

Showing Your Feminine Side

Men were Jesus' target audience, and he chose to focus on his disciples for a reason. Men like to think it was because they were special, yet the real reason could be because they had special needs. What did women then or even today in most of the world need to learn about serving or suffering, about obedience or submission? No, his message of the suffering servant was for those who needed it most, and that was men - and men are still missing the point today.

Women did not need that message, because they were already like him, or was it that Jesus lived like a woman in a man's world, without money, power or possessions? Just like a woman he showed his feelings, he cared for children, he fed the hungry and taught through story-telling; he healed the sick and was compassionate to the marginalised. In modern language, he showed his 'feminine side', which is not surprising if his genetic material came through his mother and the Holy Spirit, which was originally feminine in gender.

Showing your feminine side is just what happens to many men in midlife, and increasingly this has become the norm for younger men too.

Women needed a different message and Jesus gave it to them, and especially to one chosen woman. She knew the 'All', balancing Left and Right Sides of the New Brain, and the way to access the Mind and its powers safely. She was his confidante, perhaps also his teacher or his life partner, for Jesus was a Jew, and Jonathan Sachs affirms in his book *The Great Partnership* that there was and is no place in Judaism for celibacy.

Regardless of her marital status, Mary Magdalene was chosen by Jesus to pass on his after-life knowledge. According to her own gospel, she told the men the steps to follow to heaven, or the stages between the brain and the Mind and its miraculous powers, yet did men listen when she tried to share it with them? No, they could not believe she knew something they did not. Men were the special, chosen ones, so she was sidelined and her position denied, and this is still the position in the Church today.

It is not unknown for followers to airbrush their idol's partner out. For example, John Lennon is supposed to have once said that the Beatles were better known than Jesus, yet it was his wife who was airbrushed out of the picture in the early days of the Beatles' fame.

Without the inner, intuitive approach from the Right Side of the New Brain, the Left Side of structure and hierarchy took over the Christian Church, and the dominance of the Father continued. The original one-to-one direct relationship with God became subverted into a belief in the Christian church as the one-and-only way to God.

The feminine did make a brief re-appearance in the West during its adolescent period in chivalry and the crusades back to the old crossroads in Jerusalem, and interest was re-ignited more recently by books such as Dan Brown's *The Da Vinci Code*, but still the established Church resists re-integrating this lost knowledge or integrating women into the hierarchy. Men are still special, the only ones who can lead, and the message of the cross is twisted to fit this thinking.

Why does the image of the cross hold such power? For Jung, it was the symbol of the True Self. In earlier days a circle enclosed the cross, like the brain encircles the Wounded Body that stands at the crossroads of our brain. If we stand at the centre of the crossroads, we are integrating all the different parts of the brain, including the unconscious, and we link up with the Forebrain and those higher, so-called 'charismatic' powers above. In a slightly more familiar script, it could be imagined as being like the crew in *Star Trek* when they stand in the transporter and say: 'Beam me up Scotty!'

Standing at the crossroads of the brain's Wounded Body is the safe way to access the Mind's superhuman powers, a domain that is within everyone's reach. This is Christ's message to the world.

BRAIN WASHING

These Mind powers can, however, be downloaded without going through the protected portal of the Wounded Body. The Mind's powers or charismatic gifts come naturally to some, and can be developed and used for the benefit of others - by actors for example. Sometimes they are misused by those with a magnetic personality and the aura of glamour about them, or by someone with an over-inflated ego who fills up the unused ego space of others, using the power of words to convince us they are right. All can affect our thinking and behaviour, often so we follow them as if they were our master and we their servants, without stopping to ask why. When it is done deliberately and taken to extremes, this process is sometimes called brainwashing.

As we saw, the safest way to use the Mind's superhuman powers is through the Wounded Body of integration. In Christian terms, these powers are accessed when we have been washed clean spiritually of our sins (or lack of integration and integrity). This is very different from brainwashing, which disengages the will. However, some find a way to hack into the Mind deliberately, like hacking into a computer, to access its powers without authority.

There are also those who learn how to project onto the inner screen of others the image they want them to see, or convince them to believe what they are told, even things which are not for their benefit, calling on them to sacrifice themselves for The Man rather than the other way round - think of dictators, confidence tricksters, psychopaths, cult leaders and even some politicians. This is when the Mind's powers are used against people instead of serving them.

How do we know when someone has accessed the powers of the Mind and are using them against us? The spiritual gift called 'discernment' is given specially for that purpose, but for most of us, there is simple test. Can you use your free will to say no without being punished in some way? If you cannot, then take care. Are your individuality and rationality being bypassed or ridiculed? If so, step back, and use that individuality and rationality to break free. And most importantly, ask for help from your own Mind.

TEMPLATE

I have tried to bring ideas from the world of the Mind and spirit down to earth by using the intellectual framework we know from Integrated Thinking to see their relevance today to human development. On the spiritual path, we have to overcome the Serpent's demands and tempting offers, and then leave the tribal loyalties of the New Brain's Right Side behind for individual responsibility. After achieving success, we have to let the egotistical 'I' be crossed out at the central crossroads in the brain where there is no West or East, male or female, rich or poor, so that a new life can truly begin, and the True Self or Mind take over our brains and lives.

At some point, one might ask how, at a time when people did not even know how the organs of the body worked, did one man 2,000 years ago understand the inner world so well that he showed the stage of life psychotherapists call Self actualisation and the True Self by using his own life and body as a template - and showed us the work of the Mind too.

CHAPTER REVIEW

In this chapter, I have connected some of Christ's teaching with what is now known about the stages of human development and the Mind. Other religions have shared knowledge of the unseen world in ways that are appropriate for their time and place. All these different understandings are essential, not just as stepping-stones to the 'one and only way', but as necessary parts of the overall picture of spiritual development.

If we review the picture so far, it would seem as if an understanding of the stages in human development was originally seen as coming from a source called God and codified into religions: first there was mother nature and mother earth, the multitude of human potential in gods and goddesses; then the emergence of the dominant I AM father who becomes a loving father balancing justice with mercy, followed by the emergence and then death of the individual ego, the rise of the True Self and the realisation of the superhuman powers of the Mind. The religion we live by reflects our own and/or our society's stage of development.

At this stage, however, the integration of personal, political, global and now spiritual development within the theory of a New IT would not be complete unless we brought back into the picture all that was excluded from the understanding of the one male God as the great I AM which took over from the positive and negative aspects of gods and goddesses. What were excluded were the negative and feminine aspects as we have seen, so in Chapter 15, I will look at the negative underworld of the spiritual domain, and in Chapter 16 at the feminine aspect still largely missing from Western spiritual development today.

15 INHUMAN GLOBAL MASTERMIND

The question I want to raise here is: are all our personal, political and global failings and failures because people are mad, bad or stupid, so that we blame ourselves or others for what goes wrong? Or is there something else operating out of sight and outside our control, beyond the personal 'demons' of discarded personality traits we met earlier, which is making use of that undercover darkness in the unconscious to keep people from developing their full potential, or fuelling both sides for its own purposes like an arms dealer?

We can use the mirror of the outside world as our starting point. It seems that several underworld strands have come together via the Internet to create a global network that threatens the security of the world. Jeffrey Robinson in *The Merger* explains that, "Over recent years, a secret and deadly alliance has been formed between some of the most dangerous criminals in the world. The South American drug cartels, the Italian mafia, the Asian gangs and the Russian organised crime have stopped fighting each other and, taking lessons from the multinationals in management and organisation, have actively joined forces." Just as the authorities are doing in cyberspace, we need to separate those underworld strands in the spiritual domain, break up the networks and close the loopholes.

First we need to give a name to this spiritual force: the force is evil and one of its names is Satan. Just as human understanding of God has changed over time, so too has the role of Satan, from the Garden of Eden's Serpent, tempting us to take the quick route to higher levels of awareness, to a rather bureaucratic prosecutor of our failings. More recently, no longer content with just tempting or taunting its victims, it is sometimes portrayed as a sadistic, psychotic mastermind, ready to destroy everyone including himself rather than surrender to the authority of the law. Essentially, it seems that the forces of disintegration and destruction have stepped outside the process of integration, to set up an opposing force, the so-called 'fallen angel' or spiritual black hole.

Arthur Conan Doyle's description of Moriarty in *Memoirs Of Sherlock Holmes* is particularly apt for this underworld mastermind: "For years past I have been conscious of some power behind the malefactor, some deep organising power which for ever stands in the way of the law. Professor Moriarty is the Napoleon of crime. He is the organiser of half that is evil and nearly all that is undetected in this great city. He is a genius. He sits motionless, like a spider in the centre of its web, but that web has a thousand radiations. He only plans. But his agents are numerous and splendidly organised. The central power that uses the agent is never caught, never even suspected. He is clean-shaven, pale and ascetic looking, his face protrudes forward and is for ever slowly oscillating from side to side in a curiously reptilian fashion."

Some would say that evil is just an absence of good, but for those who have experienced its malign effect, there is also a presence, tangible and terrifying. An example between an absence and a presence may help clarify the difference. In both psychopaths and those on the autistic spectrum there is a lack of compassion but in psychopaths, there is also a presence, totally missing from those on the autistic spectrum, of a malevolent will twisted deliberately towards ill not good, covered by a deceptive facade.

In this chapter, we will look at some activities and ways of thinking which in their original purpose were for good, but which have been twisted to serve another purpose. Then, once we have separated out the strands, we will see if we can expose the mastermind itself.

SWAMPS

Like a virus hacks into a computer, evil can hack its way into the brain, and into all the systems the brain devises. James Lovelock explains in *Gaia* that, "The virus enters a living cell, commandeers its function, causing it to act out its instructions". Evil may be growing in sophistication as it absorbs more of our mental processes, like the latest computers, but it is much more than an inconvenient intruder into our thinking. Denial is one of its strongest weapons: it provides the cover for it to work unopposed and undetected.

I am going to make four propositions about what evil could be and how it could have gained access to human development; then look at how we could bring the perverted or corrupted activity back within the process of integration. The first proposition is that evil is inhuman; secondly, that it is subhuman; thirdly, that it is human, and the final proposition or possibility is that it is superhuman.

The first of the four propositions above is that it is inhuman, or perhaps pre-human might be a better description. Many of the automatic programmes in our brains and bodies contain elements pre-dating human life on earth, which evolution has adapted to human development. We have seen that the human brain does not begin at the head, and that the most primitive part, the Gut Brain, is the Serpent's 'tail', connected to the head brain through the S-shaped spinal cord.

Here in the Gut Brain, the cells are programmed by the commands of an earlier time, before light and oxygen came to the murky, swampy darkness. It is a simple, selfish programme: grow by breaking down and using any available energy source. We have looked at some examples of how this pre-human programme can become inhumane and evil when applied to people, as when people are put through the employment-mincing machine, squeezed, drained and finally discarded on the rubbish dump in the name of greater economic growth - or when disposed of in concentration camps, in ethnic cleansing, or in torture.

Bernard Bergen in *The Banality Of Evil* writes, "Never before in the history of the world had there been a government like Hitler's founding itself on a policy that its people create reality in the image of hell". We will look later at whether such a primitive programme could make the leap from gut to dominating the human brain all by itself.

We need now to look at how can we close off its entry point. We need to make sure the Gut Brain which came first pre-birth and in a child's earliest days is now last in priority, by cutting off the Serpent's tail, so that it joins forces with the Emotional Wheel. That will stop the flow to the rat run between the Gut Brain, the Serpent's autopilot of the Primal Brain and the Left Side of the New Brain. The link between them is 'bits': breaking food into bits in the stomach; the Serpent's alert arousal response that focuses on bits of the picture rather than the whole context, and the Left Side's ability to take things to bits to analyse them. On the other hand, the link between compassion in the Emotional Wheel, the Right Side's connections and the Forebrain's ability to see the bigger picture is the basis of the holistic approach.

Enclosing the Serpent within the Emotional Wheel will restrict the down-flow of energy into the Underground Pit and encourage more upward growth on the Tree of Life rather than economic growth, and that means more emphasis on people than things. This will help rebalance development of the Right Side of the New Brain in the West, and of the Forebrain globally.

AUTOMATONS

The second proposition was that evil is subhuman; if it is, then how can we protect ourselves? The human brain has been described as a series of networks, nestling inside each other like Russian dolls, but at the heart of the human brain network, there is no baby doll. It is more like a snakepit, covered by a web. From the age of cold-blooded reptiles, human beings inherited the *reptilian core*, the Serpent, which has reared its head above the Pit.

It sits on top of the spine, controlling automatic systems, including the guts, the unconscious and access to the neglected, rejected and overused parts of human development. However, we have also looked at how society has increased the Serpent's power through automation, through increasingly turning people into automatons, and the increase in various forms of artificial intelligence. Danah Zohar in *Spiritual Intelligence* states that, "As a culture we are going mad, alienated from meaning and purpose. Evil is human potential of the fragmented, decentred, spiritually stunted self".

Yet, even as automatons, people are unreliable as a means for evil to spread: they do not always clone evil by returning an eye for an eye, perpetuating revenge. Sometimes they feel compassion, even love and forgive. So now, by making use of the Primal Brain's ability to link up with other systems, evil has found a more amenable home in the global brain in cyberspace, the world wide web. It is without conscience or human control, and outside international law.

The Internet itself is not evil, only the way it can be used by those with evil intent. People are so hypnotised by the Internet's power, it has been called the 'Saviour of Mankind'. Along with the benefits that the Old IT has brought, it has created a Dark Net world where the unconscious mastermind can run rampant with its pornography, drugs and dirty dealings. The promise of automation producing more leisure seems as hollow as 'Arbeit macht frei'.

Are computers becoming more human-like or are people becoming more machine-like, living isolated, alienated lives? Richard Tarnas in *Passion Of The Western Mind* makes the comment that, "When the modern [brain] actively constructs the world as unconscious, mechanistic and impersonal, it is just then that the world is most completely a selective construct. The human [brain] has abstracted all conscious intelligence and purpose and meaning and then projected onto the world a machine".

Many now live and work in an unnatural, artificial electro-magnetic field, which is polluting our inner world and forcing our mental wavelengths to match its own hyped-up pattern, rather than working with the Mind's longer waves. In *Lifelight* Keith Foster explains how this can happen: "Everything in creation has a mirror image. The use of computers, TV, copiers, fluorescent lights and so on has created a huge web of artificial spiral vortex fields which leaches energy from organic systems, leading to the breakdown of living systems."

Our higher systems are stressed to exhaustion, and in order to survive, we fall back on the primitive autopilot of the Primal Brain and so give even more openings for lower levels to penetrate our thinking and dominate our lives. We have become almost slaves to man-made machines where time is money and money is god, rather than use things to help us progress as people.

So how do we protect ourselves? Parents can use all available devices to protect their children from the dangers of the Internet, just as they have always protected them from dangers in the real world, and governments can take steps to bring the Internet within international law. We all have to detach ourselves from being part of its network, no longer ibrains but making better use of our own brains, by seeing automation in all its forms as only a tool, not as a lifeline or an extension of ourselves. They are only extensions of the brain's auto pilot: people are so much more.

The purpose within the overall pattern of human development of automating tasks, whether to move us on from survival tasks or after acquiring new skills, is to allow people to make better use of higher levels of brain development. Then we can switch on to something much more powerful than the Internet: the untapped potential of the human brain - and Mind. We can have more face-to-face social interaction to develop the Right Side, use our imagination and creativity to develop the Forebrain, and access the world of the Mind through the mind's eye.

LOST POTENTIAL

The third proposition was that evil is human, which is probably the most painful idea to deal with because if it is inherent in people, how can we get rid of it? We have seen that everything human has its place, but that some earlier survival drives have continued to dominate past their sell-by date. I have suggested that Man the Hunter is one such drive however critical it was at earlier stages of life.

For without the hunting instinct of the sperm's tail, and the internal Big Bang of fertilisation, none of us would be here! The sperm's tail was the first guided missile, hunting down its target with deadly accuracy. Could Man the Hunter, winner takes all, "Rise to the challenge, beat the odds, the competition is standing next to you" (in chef Michael Moore's words) all be traced back to that sperm's tail?

The drive to hunt for and penetrate a target is absolutely fundamental to the creation of human life. Yet after the sperm hands over its precious goods to the much bigger egg, the tail containing the male mitochondria is discarded, its job done. So is there anything wrong with that tail worming its way back in, finger on the replay button, reliving its moment of glory? Yes, if hitting the target is all and the new life ignored, or if it is taken to extremes in the urban packs roaming the streets in search of prey, the predatory paedophile tracking his quarry. This is how evil works: it takes what is good in its place and uses it against us. So how can we turn it around without feeding its power?

We could either allow this primitive drive to continue to hold such an important position in our thinking - "miss the sales target and you're dead" - or we could follow nature and discard it. However, as with all skills developed by humanity, we do need to have some who retain the knowledge of how to hunt and shoot but only for those trained marksmen whose work is essential to human life and to maintain balance in nature, but not when killing is linked to pleasure. A better option would be to do what the brain has always done, and re-use it in a new way for further development.

Steven Pinker in *The Better Angels Of Our Nature* refers to one of the elements of violence and hunting as the predation or predatory circuit, part of the 'seeking' system, "Which neuroscientists now believe is the system that underlies wanting or craving rather than actual pleasure". If so, we could use that predatory circuit at a higher level to help us reach goals we set ourselves, so that instead of hunting, we seek out answers to questions, look for something beyond ourselves or pursue new skills, understanding or greater wisdom.

Huntress or Haunted?

Hunting is not a male drive only. The winning sperm can come from the father's smaller Y chromosome, or the larger X chromosome, which is inherited from his own mother. Dr Sarah Jarvis explains in her book *Women's Health For Life* that, "The X chromosome is much larger than the relatively puny Y chromosome". In some women, the huntress instinct turns into a scavenger, feeding on juicy tit-bits of gossip, dissecting and tearing apart reputations and relationships, like red-top newspapers.

As well as the discarded tail, when the sperm does come from the father, there is something else missing, the genetic matter from the absent fourth leg of the smaller Y chromosome. The result of this missing genetic information is that, "Males are substantially more vulnerable to a variety of developmental disorders" Peter McGuffin reported in *Nature*, 1997. Have scientists found out what women have in that extra leg that men are missing? It would seem a sensible question to ask. Some believe that what is missing is compassion, which male religious leaders have focused on as the key to the spiritual journey towards greater integration and wholeness.

It is not only men who would benefit from letting go an outdated image such as Man the Hunter. Women also have to let go something from their own basic programming, the Little Miss Perfect programme of the patiently waiting egg.

Being young, attractive, fresh, receptive is a female's earliest survival programme as the hunted target. Yet who really needs to please whom? There are millions of sperm and only one egg. Many imperfect fertilised eggs are rejected at an early stage of pregnancy, and evil regimes have tried to implement a policy of 'perfection' by getting rid of disabled people and undesirables.

This need for perfection can be misapplied by society so that girls are haunted by the fear of rejection if they show themselves as less than perfect. At a less destructive level, it can even be applied to fruit and vegetables in the shops, which have to be perfect or else they are rejected. Is it really shoppers who demand this, or something more insidious?

Challenging Outdated Programmes

The 2012 Olympics may have challenged the ideal of stick thin bodies of the pubescent female as perfection, and the 2012 Paralympics challenged the image of what it means to be disabled, yet is not just young girls who are affected by this outdated programme of perfection. What of the women who try to be everything and do everything: perfect partner, mother, worker and a perfect public image too. Needing public affirmation is a sign of something missing that the money reward system can compensate for, but does not solve the problem - but the Mind or Universal Love could.

Challenging any of these primitive programmes can be seen as a threat to our most basic survival mechanisms; they are so fundamental to life that they are protected by a firewall. We have to use our more evolved brain to recognise their place in our earliest development but also to recognise that we are all good enough, or we would not be here. Perhaps we can put the original programme to good use by encouraging prospective parents to make eggs and sperm as perfect as they can with a healthy diet, no drinking, drugs or smoking, and for us all to see that being perfect means being a perfect circle, the whole thing - good and bad, light and dark - not the either/or of linear Left Side thinking.

We have looked at three strands where there are loopholes or weaknesses which can be exploited or taken to extremes: the resistance of the Gut Brain to taking second place to more evolved stages of development; our brain's ability to link up with other systems, including artificial intelligence, and the tendency of the tail to wag the dog. All work against the upward growth in the Tree of Life.

What is really important to determine, however, is whether these and other primitive programmes do it alone. Are they really cleverer than the more evolved parts of the human brain, or is there something else that is making use of these loopholes that needs to be brought within the scope of Integrated Thinking?

INTO THE LIGHT

The final proposition was that evil is superhuman. This is probably the hardest to analyse, because it takes us out of the realm of the human brain and can leave us feeling powerless. The starting point is the Mind. The Mind operates on the longer, higher wavelengths of peace and calm. It has superhuman powers and if we ask it to, it can re-wire or re-programme our brains.

We have seen how the unconscious was designed to take any unused or overused capacity from the human system via the Serpent's trapdoor. Could this include taking some Mind powers too when we do not use them, so that its master role has been twisted in the Underground Pit into the image of the inhuman global mastermind that we call Satan?

The powers it seems to have taken over favour superhuman knowledge rather than human progress, although it can simulate compassion or fellow-feeling when required, like psychopaths. It often seems that dictators and criminal masterminds seem to be more cunning than their natural intelligence or education would suggest. It is possible that either they have tapped into the Mind's powers without authority, or are being used by the inhuman global mastermind as its puppets.

All dictators, criminal and fictional masterminds want the same thing: to be the master and take over the world. It is as if they were all from the same mould, like the stereotypes in the unconscious that we saw earlier. However, unlike the Mind that waits to be asked in, the inhuman global mastermind overrides people's wills, like dictators override the will of the people. It is possible that the word 'anti-Christ' refers to those who use the Mind's powers to destroy rather than to serve mankind.

The process of over-riding a nation's will is similar to that of over-riding an individual's will in personal abuse, beginning with the grooming and softening up process to create a connection particularly with people who have already been damaged or downtrodden, like the Germans after World War I.

Many dictators claim to feel what the people are feeling, promise better times, and offer a vision of exclusivity and being special that breaks down the boundaries between the leader and the led. Then come the small steps towards violence, which, if tolerated, escalate as the people gradually hand over their will to the leader. The title of Jean Lipman-Blumen's book is *The Allure Of Toxic Leaders* and we have to resist the attraction of their allure. One way is by following our own leader, the Mind.

Dictators seem to be able to twist the Mind's superhuman skills in intelligence, communication and healing and turn them into instruments to keep themselves in power, through their use of secret police, media control and the myth of the perfect race. They like to claim to be 'Father of their people' but in reality reduce their people to automatons: ask no questions, obey rules, and follow orders.

Some concentration camp victims even made the means of their own destruction and went sleepwalking to their destruction like automatons. Are we going to follow them, or open our eyes to the possibility that behind individual and social evils there could be something more malevolent than human failings?

There are two things that evil fears as it hides in the dark. One is the power of love in all its forms and the other is the spotlight of awareness being turned on its activities. Just as with an undeveloped negative film, exposure to the light transforms and reverses it. It can be spiritual light, the light of awareness, the light touch that lifts the spirit or the light of intellectual curiosity. "I sense that stepping into the light is a powerful metaphor for consciousness (as in birth) and for the birth of the knowing Mind", is how Antonio Damasio describes it in *The Feeling Of What Happens*.

Jung described the conscious coming-to-terms with one's Self as individuation, when an individual faces his 'shadow', all those aspects of oneself that have been denied or projected onto others. The old saying of 'use it or lose it' is true as far as it goes; what it misses out is that what we lose, something else can use for its own purposes. And that includes the powers of the Mind.

Now that we have shone a light into the darkness, and have a model for how evil may work, and how it might make use of the loopholes and imbalances in human development, we can create a viable response. Before we begin, we need a workable model of the picture of human development, including all parts of the brain, its programmes and systems, to see what is missing. This is the model I have been building through Integrated Thinking.

First and most importantly of all, we have to close off the inhuman global mastermind's supply line by asking the Mind to come into our lives for ourselves and on behalf of those too young to ask, and take control of our brains and unconscious. This means standing at the point of integration at the brain's crossroads to align oneself with the higher levels of brain development. The role of the Wounded Body at the brain's crossroads is integration, and that includes disintegration as part of the whole system, not in opposition to it. In Christian terminology this means standing at the foot of the cross and asking Christ or the Mind to take over one's brain and life.

This process is no easy task. The Primal Brain and the unconscious are creatures of habit, and when we try to change our habitual way of thinking, there is often a swift response. It can feel like you are being tempted to go back to old ways by a devil, but I prefer to think of it as being more like your computer asking, "Are you sure you want to delete this?" when you try to dump a file in the waste basket. Seen like that, we can appreciate the tempter's protective role. And of course, the bigger the changes, the stronger will be the resistance. What dictator ever gave up control willingly?

CHAPTER REVIEW

I began this chapter by asking whether all our failings are because people are mad, bad or stupid, or whether there is something else that has used gaps in people's development and awareness for its own purposes. I have tried to show the ways in which I believe a negative power, which we call evil, operates on all the levels I have proposed and can use those gaps to flourish. However, I have also tried to show that the source of its power could be taken back and used positively for higher levels of human development. This chapter may have seemed far removed from many people's experience in the West today (it is not even talked about very much in Christianity) yet in recent history and in many parts of the world today as well as in the global criminal underworld, its impact is all too clear. The negative side of spiritual development has been left to do its work unseen and unexamined for too long.

The final chapter in the book looks at what has also been left out of the picture of Western spiritual development for too long: the feminine. Can women also now be integrated back into this world as they have already entered political and global development, and help lead the way forward?

16 NEW HOPE

In the introduction to this final chapter, we will review the picture so far. We have seen how the brain seems to use itself or perhaps is used by the Mind as the template for the social, political and global worlds we have created. We have found that there is an imbalance in the West particularly between the dominance of the Primal/Left Side of the New Brain and the neglect of the Right Side/Forebrain. And the Tree of Knowledge or information-processing has for many in today's world outstripped the psychological and moral development of the Tree of Life, and this makes it harder for the Wounded Body to integrate all the different parts.

We have seen what happens when we neglect, misuse or reject parts of ourselves and how the Underground Pit operates. We have seen too how important it is to recognise different stages of development socially, politically and globally so as to move away from the Left Side division of only one right way to the idea of what is most appropriate for each stage of development. We have also considered the role of religion, the Mind and evil in our individual and collective development.

So what stage of life have people reached now where previously dominant ways of thinking need to change? Richard Tarnas in *The Passion Of The Western Mind* states that, "The history of the West has been from start to finish an overwhelmingly masculine phenomenon. But why has the pervasive masculinity of the Western intellect and spiritual tradition suddenly become so apparent to us today? I believe this is occurring only now because a civilisation cannot become conscious of itself, cannot recognise its own significance, until it is so mature that it is approaching its own death". This awareness was heightened by the Women's Movement deconstruction of patriarchal thinking.

I have suggested that death of the ego, so long associated with men, is the beginning of a new stage in human development, when the ego is transformed so it can play a supporting role in the new way of thinking, and when the female - in men and women - plays a bigger role at all levels of development.

WOMAN ALONE

There is a traditional Jewish story excluded from the Bible, like the Gospel of another go-it-alone woman Mary Magdalene, that Adam's first wife was Lilith. Lilith claimed equality with man and would not be under him, so she left Adam to be replaced by Eve the mother of men, whose own independence opened humanity's eyes to self-awareness. A return to the feminine does not mean a return to 'mother', but a new kind of woman. Lilith was the first woman to stand alone, representing women in their own right.

She has reappeared throughout history and myth, for example as Sophia or Athene, the only one of Zeus' children allowed to use his intellectual gifts, as at home in the market place as in transforming female consciousness. She is still there in public open spaces today, combining the masculine and the feminine in her full name of Pallas Athene. "She stands on public buildings as Justice, Fortitude, Wisdom and Liberty", according to Ann Shearer in *Athene*.

In mediaeval times, a woman in trade was classed as 'une femme sole'. A supreme example of a woman in her own right was Elizabeth I, the Virgin Queen, and there have been many others, mostly ignored in his-story. I have wondered if she represents the second female X chromosome that comes from her paternal grandmother via the male (the first comes from her own mother). This second X beat all the male sperm to score the goal of goals, to make it on her own.

Throughout history, there have always been women who have made it in a man's world, though their contribution has largely been ignored or 'walled-off' by man's Left Side blindness to the contributions from the other Side. Jane Robinson in *Pandora's Children* reveals some of these neglected women who in past centuries, "Were busy earning their living as engineers, plumbers, surgeons, a naval commander, Pope, pirates and a stockbroker who ran for US President". In the book she tells of, "Mercenaries, war correspondents and gold miners in South America, a spymaster from Japan, chemists and mathematicians from the Middle East, merchants and entrepreneurs from all over Europe". Today, women have made it to the highest level in the social and political world, but the spiritual world and religions are still male-dominated.

WOMEN IN SPIRIT

Today, women are creators and leaders in their own right as well as in relation to others. Women's mental and emotional development form the basis of a child's own development. "A child actually incorporates her mother's systems into her own", states Louann Brizendine. It follows that the more educated, experienced and emotionally mature a women is, the more this will benefit children and the wider society. This is why educating women has such a profound impact on the lives of those around them, fast-tracking lasting change.

We are all united through the role of women in our lives. A woman's mitochondria are passed on through the female line, while male mitochondria are discarded along with the sperm's tail. We are even more intimately linked through women, because each one of us lived in the beginning in the waters of a woman's womb and her breathing was the first wind blowing across our watery world, just as in the spiritual world, it was the breath of God, the feminine spirit called Shekinah by the Jews, that blew on the waters of the deep before the earth was born or the word was spoken.

It was our mothers who first fed us with her body and cleansed us with her blood. The placenta blood is unique; it never clots and it never stops flowing. It was this image that Jesus chose for his followers to remember him by in the wine and bread at the Last Supper. He likened himself to unleavened bread, for that is what the word placenta means - 'little bread' - and like placenta blood, his never stops flowing. Jesus, our True Self, feeds us with his body and cleanses us with his ever-flowing blood spiritually, just as a woman feeds and cleanses every baby born from a body torn in agony, yet given new life with love. When we enter a church for communion, it is like re-entering the womb to start our lives anew, re-confirming the Mind as our master.

'Christ' means the anointed one, and according to the Bible, it was a woman who anointed him with precious oil. Yet, although Christ identified himself with women's bodies, and lived life as a woman in a man's world, revealing the integrating force of the Wounded Body, what happened to women in Christianity? The image of woman was split in two, symbolised by the two Mary's: the good mother and the fallen woman, the Madonna and Whore. This split reflects a baby's early mental division between the good mother who nurtures him and the bad mother who leaves him to cry. The image of the Virgin Mary also enabled men to elevate an infantile fantasy, that a boy is the first to break his mother's barrier, into a religious dogma that excluded real women.

As I have suggested, Jesus' message of the suffering servant was mostly for men, for what did women need to learn, even today in most of the world, about suffering, obedience or serving? Learn from men, but do more than serve their needs, he told the women in his life. Think of yourselves, not others, he told the women on the way to the cross. In other words, develop your masculine, Left Side selves. He told the woman with whom he shared everything to stand alone, and to tell the men of the mysteries he had shared with her. She tried to tell them, but the other disciples would not listen to a woman, and so she cried.

WOMEN TODAY

Now it is time for women to stop crying and for men to listen. It is not the *End of Men*, the title of a book by Hannah Rosin, but it is the end of the dominance of a certain way of thinking that men have developed. It is time to integrate men and women's masculine and feminine qualities into a new way of thinking that focuses on co-operation not competition. It is also time to integrate women into all levels of social, political and spiritual development around the globe.

The freedoms that women in the West have fought for are still only a dream for many. In the Middle East according to Shereen El Feki in *Sex And The Citadel*, women's lives evoke an earlier era of the West's sexual evolution. In her review of the book in *The Times* on 23 February 2013, Janice Turner wrote that, "Their lives recall the Victorian Age, with its classic double standard, whereby men cannot have sex until marriage but cannot marry until they have sufficient means, creating a dark hinterland where prostitutes were widely used but despised."

This recalls the split I referred to earlier between images of the good mother and the fallen woman, when very early psychological stages are continued into adult thinking and externalised, causing great damage to women. Shereen El Feki's book also points out that according to a 2008 survey, 90% of married Egyptian women under 50 have suffered genital mutilation, where the clitoris is removed, to keep women sexually subservient. In denying women equality, men are denying half of themselves.

It is time to heal not only women but also the inner split between the good mother and the bad, the beautiful young princess and the rejecting matriarch. These were the archetypes into which the media and much of the public in 1997 placed Princess Diana and the Queen (and later 'Nanny' Baroness Thatcher). The deaths of Princess Diana and Baroness Thatcher allow space for another woman to emerge, not the old crone of myth, but a new integrated and mature model for woman in today's world.

Women in the West today have the money, power and possessions to help their less fortunate sisters. They own their own bodies and their own property, and they can succeed in the world of men. Hannah Rosin reports in *The End Of Men* that researcher James Chung in 2010 found that in almost all metropolitan areas, covering 91% of US population, young women had a median income higher than young men. She writes that, "The education gap is widening not just in the United States but all over the world. In 27 out of 34 industrial countries, women have more college degrees than men. The same is true in less prosperous countries." In the UK, 40% of women earn more than their male partners.

Hannah Rosin says that, "Many young women remind me of immigrants, propelled by a mysterious force to keep moving forward, trying not to think too much what would happen as all the women she knew kept swimming upstream and the men got caught in the eddies, when men became the equivalent of the family left behind in the Old Country, beloved maybe, but frustratingly left in the past".

Her message is that we need women at the top to remake the workplace and the world in their own image, an image that integrates the feminine and masculine. Yet still some hesitate to step forward. Many women have held themselves back until those less developed have matured, but women were given the greatest of all responsibilities: the future of human life on earth has always been in women's bodies. Is it now also in women's hands and brains?

Because there is no female at the highest level of our belief systems onto which the most exalted aspirations can be projected, there can be a tendency for too much to be expected of ordinary women. When they fall short, as they must, that can be an excuse for their second-class position and for men's anger against them. But whose anger against women are they really expressing, for what stands in the way of total control by the negative force? The one thing it lacks: love in all its forms, compassion, empathy and mercy and the feminine Holy Spirit of grace.

WOMEN TOMORROW

After the Mind has taken its place as our brain's master, it is the Holy Spirit according to Christianity that brings alight the particular brain networks for an individual's future work, igniting unused brain pathways, as part of a wider plan for humanity. This is called grace, the fire that comes from above not from the molten core of the past.

Sometimes these 'charismatic gifts' are new and unexpected, when a person previously had no skills in that area, but they must never be at the service of the ego, only the True Self. In her article in *The Times* on 4 April 2004, Anjana Ahuja quoted Howard Gardner as saying, "The world of the future will demand capacities that until now have been mere options".

The Holy Spirit is the spirit of holiness, wholeness and healing; it unites feminine and masculine gifts, light and dark within the whole circle, integrating gentleness and peace with conviction, commitment and the confidence for women to take their place as guardians of the flame of life, and to go out into the world as leaders, as inspiration and as a force for change. Not by women suffering, serving or sacrificing themselves and their children to the demands of the man-made world, but by moving on from the agony of a broken body giving birth into the joyfulness of spirit at the newly created life, with the love to develop it to the full.

This change, with women taking over the leading role while men reclaim their feminine side, reflects the midlife stage of human development; it also reflects the beginning of a deeper change, when the mature Forebrain takes over from the New Brain. The Forebrain is situated behind the forehead, or temples. What will be the role of outside temples when these inner temples are filled with the flowering of human potential?

Working together, men and women have the power to create themselves in a new image and to create a new world outside that reflects this inner integration, one that is filled with a sense of wholeness and hope rather than conflict.

SECTION REVIEW

This Section has been about trust, hope and the Universal Love of the Mind. But what do we do with the one great source of trust, hope and love which comes into the world every second? Millions of children die every year in the world before they are one year old because of lack of food or basic healthcare, while the weapons of violence drain a nation's resources. It may be the end of these children's short life on earth, but not the end of the human story. If we change the way we use our brains, we can re-write the human script for children and for ourselves.

Integrated Thinking follows the pattern of brain development, including finding new uses for older parts, so that previously dominant ways of thinking are not rejected but play a supporting role in future development. We need people of integrity of both genders with integrated thinking to create a new world. If we are to bring the two Trees, Knowledge and Life, information-processing and human progress, together and transform the worlds inside and out from a wasteland and into a new garden, as they have done at the Eden project or in the Olympic park, we have to reclaim and integrate the lost parts of ourselves from the Underground Pit and ask the Mind to lead us.

With integration, when the inner wall falls and becomes a bridge between male and female, West and East, rich and poor, there will be great joy, just as at a wedding. Then comes the hard work of building a new way of thinking, like building a new life in a marriage. The wall in the world outside, the Berlin Wall between West and East, came down over 20 years ago, but it is still happening inside every time an inner wall falls and becomes a bridge of understanding.

A GLOBAL MIDLIFE CRISIS?

In this book I have looked at the call for a new way of thinking by first examining what is meant by our present way of thinking, why it needs to change, who are the people who need to change and who could guide us. I have proposed Integrated Thinking, the New IT, as one way of responding to this call for change. A recurring theme in the book has been the emergence of the midlife stage of human development as an appropriate model and positive guide to these changes, one that many people can respond to personally.

The bad news is that we are facing a global crisis. Physically there will be less energy; emotionally there is fear of the future, mentally we will have to change the way we think and materially there will be less. Now for the good news. People are good at adapting to change, it is why we have survived as a species. And the really good news is that millions of people have made these changes already and have developed a new way of thinking about themselves and the world. They have survived their own crisis of change, the midlife crisis, when imbalances are corrected, the Forebrain matures, the mind's eye is opened and women move from the background to take centre stage, no longer neglected by the previously dominant Left Side of the New Brain.

Murray Stein *In Midlife* considers, "Midlife to be a time when persons are going through a fundamental shift which has a psychological and religious meaning beyond the interpersonal and social dimensions".

So is the world now facing a global midlife crisis?

AFTERWORD

I hope that people will question my hypothesis and conclusions as input from different views is all part of Integrated Thinking. However, I will try to address some questions here that may occur to people as they read this book:

1. Explanation or excuse?

Are people responsible for their actions and consequences when so much seems to be either pre-programmed or outside their control? Being unaware of the forces and processes that affect our thinking and behaviour is a defence in mitigation, yet once these processes are made conscious, then people have a responsibility, with professional support, for making reparation for their past actions, and for their future behaviour and decisions.

2. Recommendations

This is not a self-help book of prescriptive lists of things to do to guarantee success, nor a scientifically proven thesis. It is more in the nature of a persuasive argument. There are, however, some general guidelines that have emerged that people can apply to their own lives:

1. Rebalance the Left and Right Sides of the New Brain in whatever way is appropriate to one's time and place
2. Reverse the relative importance of Primal Brain/Forebrain
3. Reclaim the neglected parts from the Underground Pit
4. Refer to the Mind for answers and guidance.

We all have a Mind as an inner guide and it is the Mind that will show the way ahead, once we have accessed its powers safely as I have described in Chapter 14.

The Mind will also answer any questions and the responses can come in many forms - a line in a book that stands out, an unexpected coincidence, a meaningful dream, a person who appears at the right moment, an inner voice. We can also look to our own lives, our relationships, work, beliefs, interests, even our pets, to see reflections of our inner world and what the next step might be.

3. How do we know?

How do we know which voice we are listening to, is it the unconscious, the ego or just habit, is it really our inner guide - or are we going mad? The usual test is to see what are the consequences or 'fruits' of listening to that voice and see who would benefit. I usually find it is the quiet voice that sometimes struggles to be heard that has my best interests at heart, especially when it is something that my own ego does not want to do.

4. How do I know?

I began working on this theory at a time when there was far less research on the brain, so how did I gain knowledge that was outside my own personal experience? Until 25 years ago, I thought that knowledge was passed down through parents, teachers, books and television, with the occasional flash of inspiration. Then I was shown another source of knowledge, which came into my head unasked, but after many years of trying to understand painful personal experiences. I found that just as computers can teach us how to use them, so our Minds could teach us about our brains. By asking Christ to take over my life, I was given knowledge of subjects outside my own experience and even of subjects I had no name for. Before the age of books and computers, the Mind-brain link was how people discovered and explored their inner and outer worlds. This book is the result of my own inner discovery, rewritten and revised over many years, as I tried to incorporate the changes I understood intellectually into the reality of my own life and to make the knowledge accessible to all.

REFERENCES

Amen, D (2009) Change Your Brain, Change Your Life *Piatkus*

Arden J (2010) Rewire Your Brain *John Wiley& Sons*

Armstrong, K (2000) Battle For God *HarperCollins*

Armstrong, K (2011) 12 Steps To A Compassionate Life *Bodley Head*

Arrowsmith-Young, B (2012) The Woman Who Changed Her Brain *Square Peg*

Ashdown, P (2007) Swords And Ploughshares *Orion*

Bainbridge, D (2009) Teenagers *Portobello Books*

Bainbridge, D (2009) Middle Age *Portobello Books*

Baron-Cohen, S (2011) Zero Degrees Of Empathy *Allen Lane*

Barr, D (2013) Maggie And Me *Bloomsbury Publishing*

Batchelor, S (2004) Living With The Devil *Riverhead Books*

Bergen, B (1998) The Banality Of Evil *Rowmen & Littlefield*

Blair, T (2010) Tony Blair: A Journey *Hutchinson*

Brizendine, L (2006) The Female Brain *Bantam*

Brown, D (2003) The Da Vinci Code *Corgi*

Bruges, J (2007) The Big Earth Book *Alastair Sawday*

Carter, R (2000) Mapping the Mind *Phoenix*

Chopra, D (2000) How To Know God *Rider*

Chopra, D (2012) Superbrain *Rider*

Cohen, G (2005) The Mature Mind *Basic Books*

Connelly, D (1979) Traditional Acupuncture: The Law Of The 5 Elements *Centre For TA*

Conway, E (2009) 50 Economic Ideas You Really Need To Know *Quercus*

Cook, M (2002) Lords Of Creation *Robson Books*

Crawford, M (2010) Creating a Forest Garden *Green Books*

Damasio, A (1994) Descartes' Error *Papermac*

Damasio, A (2000) The Feeling Of What Happens *Vintage*

Denning, Lord (1984) Landmarks Of The Law *Butterworth& Co*

Doidge, N (2008) The Brain That Changes Itself *Penguin Books*

Doyle, A C (reprint 1981) Memoirs of Sherlock Holmes *Penguin Books*

Dweck, C (2012) Mindset *Constable & Robinson*

Eposito, J (1999) The Islamic Threat *OUP*

El Feki, S (2013) Sex And The Citadel *Chatto & Windus*

Faludi, S (2007) The Terror Dream *Atlantic Books*

Fine, C (2006) A Mind Of Its Own *Icon*

Foster, K (1997) Lifelight *Sagax*

Freeman, S (2009) Binge Trading *Penguin Books*

Glenny, M (2011) Dark Market *Bodley Head*

Goleman, D (1996) Emotional Intelligence *Bloomsbury Publishing*

Gore, A (2007) The Earth In Balance *Earthspan*

Greenfield, S (2008) The Quest For Identity in 21st Century *Sceptre*

Hammond, R (2001) Emergence *MacMillan*

Hawker, P (1998) Soul Survivor *Northstone Publishing Inc*

Hefferman, M (2012) Wilful Blindness *Simon & Schuster*

Howatch, S (1987-) The Starbridge Series *Fontana*

James, O (2007) Affluenza *Vermilion*

Jamison, C (2008) Finding Happiness *Weidenfeld & Nicolson*

Jarvis, S (2010) Women's Health For Life *Dorling Kindersley*

Johnson, S (2001) Emergence *Penguin*

Jones, S (2013) The Serpent's Promise *Little, Brown Book Group*

De Kerckhove, D (1995) The Skin Of Culture *Kogan Page*

Klein, M (1988) Love, Guilt and Reparation *Virago*

Kubler-Ross, E (1969) On Death And Dying *Simon & Schuster*

Kurzweil, R (1999) The Age Of Spiritual Machines *Phoenix*

Lammy, D (2011) Out Of The Ashes *Guardian*

Lanchester, J (2010) Whoops *Allen Lane*

Lanier, J (2013) Who Owns The Future? *Allen Lane*

Lasch, C (1984) The Minimal Self *Picador*

Laslo, E (2002) You Can Change The World *Positive News Publishing Ltd*

Le Fanu, J (2009) Why Us? *Harper Press*

Lehrer, J (2009) The Decisive Moment *Canongate*

Lind, M (2003) Made In Texas *Basic Books*

Lipman-Blumen, J (2005) Allure Of Toxic Leaders *OUP*

Lovelock, J (2001) Gaia *Gaia*

Maas, P (2009) Crude World *Allen Lane*

Macfarlane, A (2005) Letters To Lily *Profile*

Maclean, P (1990) The Triune Brain In Evolution *Greenwood Publishing Group*

McGilchrist, I (2009) The Master And His Emissary *Yale University Press*

Malloch-Brown, M (2011) The Unfinished Global Revolution *Allen Lane*

Mamen, M (2005) Pampered Child Syndrome *Kingsley Publishers*

Marr, A (2007) A History Of Modern Britain *Macmillan*

Marr, A (2012) Diamond Queen *Pan Books*

Maslow, A (1998) Towards A Psychology Of Being *John Wiley & Sons*

Milne, D (2004) Coping With A Midlife Crisis *Sheldon*

Moore, M (2011) Blood Sugar *New Holland Publishers*

Morgan, N (2005) Blame My Brain *Walker Bros*

Morozov, E, (2013) To Save Everything, Click Here *Penguin Books*

Nisbett, R, (2003) Geography of Thought *Nicholas Brealey*

Neuberger, J (2005) The Moral State We're In *Harper Collins*

Odent, M (1986) Primal Health *Century Hutchinson*

Odent, M (1999) The Scientification of Love *Free Association*

Pallardy, P (2006) Gut Instinct *Rodale*

Palmer, S (2006) Toxic Childhood *Orion*

Palmer, S (2009) 21st Century Boys *Orion*

Pinker, S (2011) The Better Angels Of Our Nature *Allen Lane*

Porritt, J (2007) Capitalism *Earthscan*

Read, N (2005) Sick And Tired *Weidenfeld & Nicolson*

Ridley, M (2010) The Rational Optimist *Fourth Estate*

Robinson, J (2002) Pandora's Children *Constable*

Robinson, J (1999) The Merger *Simon & Schuster*

Rosin, H (2012) The End of Men *Penguin Viking*

Sacks, J (2011) The Great Partnership *Hodder & Stoughton*

Schultz, M L (2005) The New Feminine Brain *Atria Books*

Schwartz, J (2002) The Mind And The Brain *Regan Books*

Seldon, A (2007) Blair Unbounded *Simon & Schuster*
Shearer, A (1996) Athene *Viking Arkana*
Sheey, G (1999) Passages In Men's Lives *Simon & Schuster*
Smith, D (2010) The Age Of Instability *Profile Books*
Solomon, J & G (1998) Harry Oldfield's Invisible Universe *Thorsons*
Soros, G (2000) Open Society *Little Brown & Co*
Stein, M (1983) In Midlife *Spring Publications*
Stevens, A C (1994) Jung *Oxford Press*
Talbott, S (1995) The Future Does Not Compute *O'Reilly*
Tarnas, R (1991) Passion Of The Western Mind *Pimlico*
Taylor, M (1999) Star Trek *Pocket Books*
Taylor, S (2010) Waking From Sleep *Hay House*
Tolle, E (2000) A New Earth *Michael Joseph*
Tuchman, B (1978) A Distant Mirror *Macmillan*
Tuchman, B (1984) The March of Follies *Abacus*
Twenge, J and Campbell K (2010) The Narcissism Epidemic *Simon & Schuster*
De Waal, F (2005) Our Inner Ape *Granta*
Weed, S (1992) The New Menopause Years
Western, D (2007) The Political Brain *Public Affairs*
Wise, J (2009) Extreme Fear *Palgrave Macmillan*
Zohar, D (2000) Spiritual Intelligence *Bloomsbury*

ACKNOWLEDGEMENTS

Thank you to all who have been a part of my life, especially those who have accompanied me along sections of the way, those who have supported and advised me, those who have doubted and challenged me, and above all, those who have taken me into their homes. I am forever grateful. I also want to thank all the writers whose books have kept me company these long and often lonely years. And I certainly could not have done my work without the support of my daughters, their families and my friends, especially Joy, Dave and Aileen.

Thank you also to those who helped in the preparation of this book: Mike and Penny for the drawings, Jan and Susan for their comments and to Jan for help with the cover layout. A particular thank you too to Dietrich and David who supported me in my early conference ventures.

Bless you Sarah and James for your prayers that have sustained and protected me.

Finally, I have tried to be faithful to the trust placed in me to share this knowledge, but the mistakes are my own.

Sue Pearson has worked in business, studied law and
psychology and has managed community projects.
She has four grandchildren and lives in Devon.
This is her first published book.